THE EXCAVATION OF STE MARIE I

Glass vessel made in Venice between 1590 and 1600. Brought to
Ste Marie by the Jesuits.

KENNETH E. KIDD

THE

EXCAVATION

OF

STE MARIE I

UNIVERSITY OF TORONTO PRESS
1949

Copyright, Canada, 1949
University of Toronto Press
Reprinted 2017
ISBN 978-1-4875-9228-8 (paper)
London: Geoffrey Cumberlege
Oxford University Press

Preface

THIS report sets forth the results of the excavation of the site
known as Ste Marie I on the Wye River, near Midland, Ontario.
It is hoped that it will be in some measure a contribution to our
knowledge of a small but important episode in Canadian history;
namely, the activities of the Jesuit Fathers in the decade of their
residence among the Huron Indians. The results may indeed have
an interest outside Canada, since the Huron area was one of the
most thickly populated regions of Indian settlement in North
America in the early seventeenth century, and in recent years
there has been a growing interest in the possibilities of archaeological research for the study of such regions. In the decade of
their residence among the Hurons, the Jesuits attempted to build
a native commonwealth founded on Christian belief: an attempt
which was suddenly and utterly ended by the Iroquois raids of
1649. The very heart and core of this famous enterprise was the
establishment called by the Jesuits themselves Ste Marie.*
Hitherto, knowledge of it has been confined to what could be
learned from written records; this can now be augmented,
especially in regard to its physical aspects, with the information
obtained by means of archaeology, and presented in this report.

Since the amount of historical archaeology which has been
done in North America is still rather inconsiderable, each field
worker has had to devise many of his own procedures, while
following in general established techniques. This has certainly
been true of work at Ste Marie.

Although no adequate expression of thanks can here be given,
the author is glad to acknowledge his indebtedness for assistance
of many kinds. It was owing to the vision of Dr. C. T. Currelly,
one-time director of the Royal Ontario Museum of Archaeology,
that the Museum was enabled to perform the service of excavating
Ste Marie I, and for this much credit is due him. To Professor

*The place is now known as Ste Marie I, to distinguish it from a second Ste
Marie, located on Christian Island.

T. F. McIlwraith, associate director of the same institution, the writer wishes to acknowledge his gratitude for unfailing support at all times and for his patient help and criticism of the manuscript in its various stages of preparation. Professor H. A. Thompson, formerly assistant director, has given liberally of his wide experience; his suggestions for the better presentation of material have greatly enhanced the usefulness of the report. To Miss W. Needler, Miss B. Maw, Miss M. Thomson, and Mr. J. H. Classey is due most of the credit for field work, such as recording, cataloguing, photography, and a goodly share of excavating, particularly of the more detailed sort. They have also contributed much to the results by identifying material, and in preparing plans, line drawings, and other detailed work, without which this report could not have been produced. Various other members of the Museum staff have also made direct contributions to the work. Mr. F. St. G. Spendlove rendered valuable assistance in identifying remains, particularly of the Venetian glass, and Miss D. K. Macdonald in analysing the weave of textile remains. Mr. Wm. Todd, Museum preparator, not only achieved a marvel of reconstruction in his work on the Venetian glass, but completed many less spectacular but equally painstaking jobs. For all of this assistance, the writer is much indebted.

The Department of Highways for Ontario made a most valuable contribution by laying out a survey of the site, under the able direction of Mr. N. D. Bennett. The help of Dr. D. F. Putnam, Department of Geography in the University of Toronto, and of Mr. L. J. Chapman, Ontario Research Foundation, in the matter of soil structure and geology, was likewise of great assistance.

To the Jesuit Order and particularly to the Reverend T. J. Lally, S. J., a debt of great magnitude is due for their abundant kindness and hospitality to all members of the Museum party, and for their help with equipment and resources. The author knows that even when these were urgently needed elsewhere, the Order gladly and willingly put them at the disposal of the excavators. He is happy to avail himself of this opportunity of thanking the Jesuit Order and his kind host, Father Lally, for their assistance and hospitality. For permission to study the manuscript of Father

Martin, an earlier student of the site, in the archives of St. Mary's College, Montreal, grateful acknowledgement is made to the Jesuit Order and in particular to Father Paul Desjardins, S. J., the College archivist. Special thanks are due to Father Lally and to Father Hourigan for their careful reading of the manuscript and for their valuable comments and suggestions.

Research of the kind connected with Ste Marie inevitably draws upon many fields of specialization. So diverse indeed have been the sources from which help has been drawn that it is not possible to acknowledge them all in detail, but they are nevertheless gratefully received. Special thanks, however, are extended to the following: to Miss Lillian Payne and Mr. Wilfred Bell who spent considerable time and effort on the excavation; to Miss M. Tremaine, then of the Toronto Public Library, for valuable bibliographical suggestions; to Dr. G. M. Stanley, Department of Geology, University of Michigan, for important information concerning the geology of the Georgian Bay region; to Father Desjardins, St. Mary's College, and Mr. Wilfrid Jury, University of Western Ontario, for help in identification of remains; to Dr. C. W. Jefferys, Toronto for valuable suggestions concerning architectural problems; to Dr. H. B. Sifton, Department of Botany, University of Toronto, and his staff, for work in identifying plant remains; to Dr. John Oughton, then of the Royal Ontario Museum of Zoology, and now of the Ontario Agricultural College, for identifying molluscs; to Messrs. Leslie Prince, S. Downing, and C. E. Hope of the above Museum for their work in identifying fish, bird, and mammal bones; and to Dr. A. C. Whitford, Newburgh, N.Y., for examining textile fibres.

To a host of others, too numerous to be mentioned individually, and to the staff of Fort Ste Marie Inn who helped in no small way to make our stay comfortable and pleasant, a debt of gratitude is owed.

K. E. K.

Contents

List of Illustrations

DISTRIBUTION PLAN

PLATES

THE EXCAVATION OF STE MARIE I

I. Introduction

HISTORICAL BACKGROUND

THE tragic story of Ste Marie I is well known in Canadian history. Begun by the Jesuits in the year 1639 as a centre for their activities among the Huron Indians, the mission lasted but a brief decade; in 1649 it was abandoned and burned by the Jesuits themselves. The reason, of course, was the destruction and dispersion of the Hurons in that year by attacks of unprecedented fury unleashed against them by the Five Nations Iroquois. With the Hurons gone, the Jesuits had no alternative but to depart from the land. The entire story is brilliantly told by Francis Parkman in *The Jesuits in North America.*

The choice of Ste Marie and of the Huron country as a centre for missionary activity was no accident. For nearly thirty years previous to the founding of Ste Marie, Huronia had been visited and close contacts had been established there by French fur traders, explorers, and missionaries. In the early years of French settlement on the St. Lawrence, fleets of Huron canoes had come to Quebec, first perhaps from curiosity to see the white man, then to engage in trade. Soon they came with regularity and in increasing numbers. Thus before a white man visited Huronia, the Huron Indians were doubtless well acquainted with the benefits of European trade goods, and knew the appearance of the strangers from across the great water. Champlain, in 1615, visited the land of the Hurons, and almost on the same day the Recollet priest, Joseph Le Caron, arrived from Quebec by a slightly different route; there is, indeed, some uncertainty about which can claim priority. Champlain remained the better part of a year with the Hurons, even travelling with them to visit the Petuns, a kindred tribe which lived twenty or thirty miles to the west, and accompanying them on a raiding expedition against the Five Nations. The Recollets stayed on in the country after Champlain's departure and established missions among the Hurons; these they continued to administer until 1626. In that year, they turned over the missionary work to the Jesuit Order. The redoubtable Jesuit, Jean de Brébeuf, at that time first entered the country which was to be the scene of his heroic labours and his martyrdom. After him came a score or more members of his Order, who established several missions in such Huron villages as Ossossané or "La Rochelle," Scanonaenrat or "St. Ignace," and Teanaostaiaë or "St. Joseph."

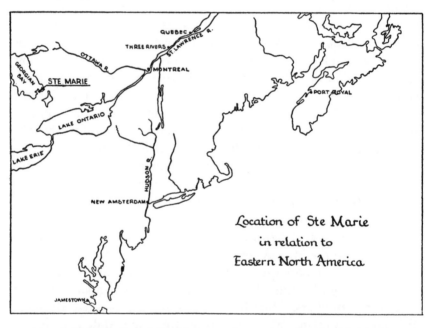

MAP 1. The location of Ste Marie in relation to eastern North America.

The advantages of Huronia as a French base rested upon a variety of geographical, economic, and cultural factors. Situated between the Severn River and Lake Simcoe on the east, Georgian Bay on the north, and Nottawasaga Bay on the west, Huronia was but a tiny area in itself. Nevertheless, it possessed strategic importance, lying as it did so close to the heart of the continent and on the direct route to the interior. Lake Huron lay before it, while far to the west was Lake Michigan, and beyond the straits of Mackinaw stretched the vast expanse of Lake Superior whose existence at that time was hardly suspected by the French. Huronia was almost the farthest west known land—the most distant outpost that could be maintained under the existing system of communications. As it was situated at the edge of the great Laurentian Shield, its inhabitants, the Huron Indians, were in a position to control traffic to the western fur country, which was bound to yield a vast revenue to the holders of this bottle-neck through which trade must pass. Westward, all rivers flowed either north or south into Lake Superior or Lake Michigan; only one flowed from east to west. This vitally important artery was held in firm control by Huron vassals, the Nipissings, whose name it bears. By ascending it, connection could be made with the Mattawa and the Ottawa Rivers and thereby with the St. Lawrence. Thus there was at hand a not-too-difficult route from Georgian Bay to Quebec itself.

The Great Lakes system was then but dimly comprehended. It was realized that there must be good fur country around its western extremities, and that a potential water route for transpor-tation was at hand. Though Lakes Huron, Erie, and Ontario seemed to afford some protection against enemies, particularly against the Five Nations who lived in what is now New York State, they were not used, nor useful, as water routes in them-selves. Lake Ontario in particular was avoided by the Hurons because it was dominated by the Five Nations who occupied its farther shore. When they wished to visit it, as they sometimes did, the Trent Valley system of rivers and lakes gave easy access. Leading to Quebec there was still another route which, though not commonly recognized, could be and apparently was used by the Hurons. This cannot be defined with exactitude, but it ap-pears to have followed the Ottawa River past Lake Timiskaming, Grand Lake, and the Gatineau River, eastward to Bell River, and through a chain of lakes and rivers to the tributaries of Lake St. John. Thence it was possible to reach the headwaters of the St. Maurice River and finally the St. Lawrence itself. Such a route, Hunt assures us, was consistently used by the Huron traders.* A nation thus in command of useful water routes, and in a posi-tion to monopolize the lucrative fur trade, was well worthy of cultivation by the French.

The Hurons seem to have become, to a considerable extent,

*G. T. Hunt, *Wars of the Iroquois* (Madison, Wisc., 1940), p. 60.

a nation of traders. Though agriculture was their basic industry, it was carried on chiefly by the women, leaving the men free to engage in the fur trade; and its abundant yield furnished a surplus which could be used in exchange for furs, meats, and other necessities which the Huron country no longer provided. Hence the furs that the Hurons could not afford to buy outright, they could control by other means. The Neutrals, to give only one example, had a volume of surplus furs which they could release in trade, but the Hurons, according to Hunt, exercised such a suzerainty over them that they were forced to route their surplus through Huron channels. The Petuns were in a similar position. As for the nations farther west and north, they had of necessity to reckon with the Hurons and their allies, such as the Nipissings, who controlled the French River-Lake Nipissing route. Only the Allumettes on the Ottawa River dared, more or less successfully, to question the authority of the Hurons; but by so doing, they isolated and alienated themselves from all their neighbours.

Although the Hurons' monopoly of the fur trade made them useful allies of the French and was a cause of the establishment of the Jesuit missions in Huronia, it also provoked the hostility of the Five Nations Indians against the Hurons, and this rivalry eventually resulted in the destruction of Huronia and the abandonment of the French missions there. The Five Nations and the Hurons, alike in linguistic, cultural, and economic respects, found themselves diametrically opposed on the fur-trade issue. Situated as the Five Nations were athwart the Albany and the Hudson, they could have controlled an important segment of the trade between the western tribes and the English and Dutch on the coast, had not the Hurons diverted it into French channels before it had a chance to reach them. Rivalry and then animosity ran high. Vainly did the Five Nations strive to arrange by treaty with the French and the Hurons to share the fur trade; only when they found the treaties dishonoured and ever larger flotillas of Huron fur cargoes reaching Quebec in 1646 did they resort to other and stronger methods of persuasion. Hunt sums up the matter tersely: "The Hurons had the furs, they refused to give them up peacefully, therefore they were destroyed."[*] He feels

[*] Hunt, *Wars of the Iroquois*, p. 54.

that any other tribe in the same situation would have done precisely as did the Five Nations.

Culturally, the Hurons were much above any of the other tribes with whom the French had come in contact. A numerous, settled, agricultural people, they offered the missionaries at least a reasonable prospect of some stability. Since they were not only self-supporting, but had a surplus of food for trading purposes, they were not likely to make heavy drains upon French resources. The Jesuits themselves stress the fact that the sedentary nature of the Hurons was one of the principal reasons for choosing Huronia as a field for missionary enterprise. It should be noted, however, that up to 1639 the French had scarcely come into contact with the Neutral Indians who were almost equally well situated, for the simple reason that the Hurons tried to prevent such meetings, in order to control the trade.

The basis of Huron agriculture was Indian corn, with beans, squash, and sunflowers important additions. These, with tobacco for smoking, were the only cultivated plants. Fields were worked until the soil became exhausted, and this practice, combined with the depletion of the wood supply, resulted in the custom of moving villages to new sites every ten or twelve years. Thus in a single generation an entire village, the population of which was astoundingly large, would move at least twice.* Fish was a popular food, but meat seems to have been scarce. Furs for clothing were none too abundant. Houses were box-like affairs, 50 or 100 feet long, with partitions dividing them into several rooms, each room being the home of one family. These "longhouses" were usually covered with elm-bark.

Descent was reckoned in the maternal line, and in other matters also, women occupied positions of some authority and respect. Councils were regularly instituted, and conducted according to a strict procedure; Brébeuf points out that the speakers even used a special intonation, reminding one of the similar custom among our own speech-makers. Embassies to foreign nations were frequently dispatched. On such occasions, the "speaker" took with him a number of strings of wampum or

---

*This practice of moving villages periodically has resulted in a far larger number of village sites in Huronia than would otherwise have been the case.

shell beads, which served as mnemonic devices; the giving and the acceptance of these rendered proceedings legal and binding. Though the language was not written, it was so well known to surrounding tribes that a Huron seldom needed an interpreter. Numerous ceremonies occupied much of the time of the Hurons; some of them were official proceedings, but more often they were of a social or shamanistic character. The working of wood and stone, the making of shell and bone ornaments, trade, hunting and fishing, and the building of fortifications fell to the lot of the men. In addition to tilling the fields and gathering firewood, the women were responsible for cooking, attending to the children and household duties, making pottery vessels, gathering hemp for the manufacture of bags and fish nets, and making the clothes. In times of need, the Hurons shared freely with their fellows and the fields were held to be common property. Yet in private matters, they exhibited a high appreciation of property; they were greedy, covetous, and grasping.

The population at the time of the first entrance of the French was large. The Jesuits frequently spoke of it as having been around 30,000 previous to 1636; after that date, smallpox and other diseases reduced it by half. If these estimates are correct, the Hurons were by far the most numerous tribe in the northeast, twice as populous as the Five Nations. The Neutrals and the Petuns had probably about the same population as the latter.

The large numbers and comparative stability of the Hurons influenced the Jesuits to select them for their missionary work. They had experimented with such peoples as the nomadic Algonkian tribes north and west of Quebec and had found the results unsatisfactory and discouraging. The settled Hurons, who would not be off to the woods at the first sign of spring, offered better prospects of success. Their ideal seems to have been to establish among the wealthiest, most populous tribe in the interior, a kind of native commonwealth, French in culture and Catholic in religion.

Beginning in a small way, the Jesuits struggled to increase the number of their missions and attendants. It was their practice to send a priest to each of the largest towns to live and carry on missionary work among its inhabitants and those of its satellite

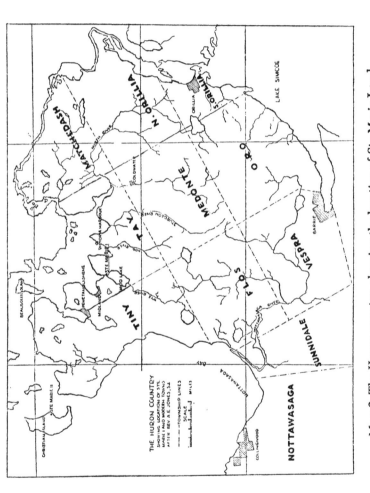

MAP 2. The Huron country, showing the location of Ste Marie I and modern towns. After A. E. Jones, S. J.

villages. Through time, the missionaries increased in numbers, as did their wants. They especially needed a place to which they could retire from the asperities of Huron life for a time, and where they could read, meditate, and converse with men of their own language and culture upon common problems.

In 1639, the leading spirits among the Jesuits determined to begin the construction of such a place, and for the purpose chose as central a location as possible with respect to the surrounding mission towns. As Father Jones has expressed it, "The new Superior, F. Jérôme Lalemant, concluded to adopt a system of concentration, and establish a permanent central Residence, quite independent of, and remote from any existing village, and thence to send the Fathers out on flying missions to the several Indian towns."* The carefully chosen site, accessible from all parts of the country and yet easily defended, was on the east side of the Wye River about a mile from its mouth. Father Lalemant describes it in the *Relation* for 1640 as "situated in the middle of the country, on the shore of a beautiful river which, being not more than a quarter of a league in length, joins together two lakes,—one which extends to the West, verging a little toward the North, which might pass for a freshwater sea; the other, which is toward the South, the contour of which is hardly less than two leagues."† The latter is now known by the unromantic name of Mud Lake and is little more than a marsh. A few acres of open water do exist, but most of it is choked with pickerel weed, water lilies, and water sedges. River and lake lie in a small level plain hemmed in by low rolling hills. Near the upper end of the river, 500 feet north of Mud Lake, there is a small headland of drier ground, narrowing toward the marsh. Here the Fathers chose to build. North of the site stands a high hill, commanding an excellent view of both the countryside and of Georgian Bay. The land east of the headland is at present scarcely better than a marsh; whether it was forested in the seventeenth century is impossible to say.

At one time, most of the Huron country was covered by a

*A. E. Jones, *Old Huronia* (Toronto, 1908), p. 313.

†R. G. Thawaites (ed.), *The Jesuit Relations and Allied Documents* (73 vols., Cleveland, 1896-1901), vol. XIX, pp. 133-5.

prehistoric lake, the present hilltops standing out of it as small islands. As the lake shrank, it left successive shorelines which may still be seen. Silt which entered it was laid down at its bottom in layers, each layer corresponding to a flood season; these varves, as they are technically called, may be seen clearly in the land around Ste Marie.* New drainage paths opened up and, approximately 4,000 years ago, the old lake receded to the present limits of Lake Huron.

The site chosen for Ste Marie is not one that would be likely to appeal to modern ideas. In those days, however, and indeed until quite recent times, low-lying land, being considered warmer than more exposed locations, was favourably regarded for building purposes. The mosquitoes must have been a constant torment, and the danger of flooding considerable. However, as Lalemant observes, the headland provided good garden prospects; and the buildings, once constructed, would be within easy distance of the water and could be defended with less effort than if they stood in a more exposed position. The determining factors in its selection, however, were undoubtedly its central position with regard to Huron territory and its easy accessibility.

Construction was begun sufficiently early in 1639 so that the buildings might be occupied in the summer of that year. Simultaneously, La Rochelle and St. Joseph II were abandoned as residences, a fact which moved the author of the last-mentioned *Relation* to observe that "thus we have now in all the country but a single house which is to be firm and stable,—the vicinity of the water being very advantageous to us for supplying the want, in these regions, of every other vehicle; and the lands being fairly good for the native corn, which we intend, as time goes on, to harvest for ourselves."

The work of construction must have presented extraordinary difficulties. The French, it will be remembered, were 800 miles from their base of supplies in Quebec—a fact which permitted the importation of very few skilled labourers and of only the most indispensable materials such as metal goods. All else had to be procured from the country. Timber and masonry requirements were readily obtained. Labour, recruited from the native popula-

*See Fig. 1, p. 32.

tion, must have been unsatisfactory. Yet in 1639 we are told that
"a single house" was already in existence. We are safe in assuming
that, as time passed, additions and improvements were made
commensurate with the needs and resources of the settlement.
For instance, the number of visiting Indians in 1642 made it
necessary to build a hospice for their use. By the end of 1644,
according to the *Jesuit Relations*, the Fathers had "been com-
pelled to establish a hospital there for the sick, a cemetery for the
dead, a church for public devotions, a retreat for pilgrims, and
finally, a place apart from others, where the infidels . . . who are
only admitted by day when passing that way . . . can always
hear some good word respecting their salvation. The hospital is
so distinct from our dwelling that not only men and children,
but even women, can be admitted to it." The "hospital" here
referred to must have been enclosed within the compound which
nineteenth-century observers describe as having existed south of
the residence. This place is said to have been protected by an
earthwork which swung crescent-like from the southeast corner
of the fortified area west and south to the river's bank. (Maps
3, 4, 5.)

During its decade of existence, the Residence of Ste Marie I
was a place of retreat for the missionaries as well as a centre for
the diffusion of European culture. While missionary work was
the primary concern of its inhabitants, real attempts were made
by Brébeuf and his fellow priests to introduce to the Hurons such
new customs as the raising of domestic animals, to which end
calves, pigs, chickens, turkeys, and pigeons were imported; the
cultivation of new vegetables and fruits; and perhaps also the
manufacture of pottery in the European style, and other crafts
formerly not known to them. In addition, the priests at Ste Marie
attempted to provide medical and surgical care, so far as lay in
their power; other "social services" also had their Canadian
beginnings here.

The number of Europeans sheltered within the walls of Ste
Marie increased with the years. In 1645, fifty-eight Frenchmen,
including six boys, three domestics, and twenty-two soldiers—
the largest population of the decade—were in residence there.
Aside from the construction necessitated by the pressure of

enemies, this increasing population in itself would have demanded enlargement of the facilities at Ste Marie. On these matters, however, the *Jesuit Relations* throw scant light.

The storm of the Iroquois raids broke in the winter of 1648-9, when a large band of enemy warriors infiltrated into the Huron country and with masterly strategy isolated and destroyed the settlements one after another. The largest village of all, St. Joseph II, was the first to be attacked; its resistance proved utterly futile. One by one the Huron villages fell. The Jesuit priests who were resident in them refused to leave and died as martyrs. Brébeuf and Lalemant were captured at St. Louis and then taken to St. Ignace where they were slain on March 17, 1649. Within a few months the Hurons were a broken people.

The Residence of Ste Marie I was never attacked, for what reason we do not know. The surviving Frenchmen congregated there to plan the next step. Among other things, they collected and buried there the remains of their martyred brothers. On March 21, 1649, the surviving Hurons betook themselves to the comparative safety of Christian Island, some eight miles offshore from the Penetanguishene Peninsula. Since the mission field was now practically depopulated and was likely to remain in that condition for years to come, the Fathers realized that it was pointless to remain in the country. Accordingly they collected together at Ste Marie I their most useful or most valuable possessions, built rafts and a small vessel, and set fire on May 15 to the Residence they had built and in which they had put such high hopes. On June 14 they sailed with their possessions to Christian Island to join their Huron friends. They also took with them the larger bones of the martyrs.*

The French and the Hurons spent the following year on the Island. Apparently it was their original intention to make it a permanent settlement, for the Jesuits immediately began to construct a second "residence" which they named Ste Marie II. However, lack of provisions and a complete crop failure brought untold hardship during the ensuing winter. In the spring of 1650, everyone agreed that the place must be abandoned. Accordingly, the final dissolution of the Jesuit missions in Huronia took place;

*The smaller bones were presumably re-interred.

the Hurons dispersed and the priests sought new fields. Ste Marie II was abandoned on June 10, 1650.

Very little is known of the history of Ste Marie I from the time of the exodus until the coming of European settlers in the late eighteenth and early nineteenth centuries. It is probable that groups of Iroquois made use of their newly acquired territory as occasion demanded. From time to time, bands of Algonkian Indians presumably came down from the north to hunt, fish, or make their way to trading posts. This would be particularly true as time went on, and their fear of the Iroquois lessened. Indeed, during this period, extensive movements and new alignments seem to have taken place among the Algonkian nations of the Great Lakes area. Eventually some of them settled in the old homeland of the Hurons; the white settlers encountered them there and identified them with the Ojibwa (Chippewa).* Whether these people made any use of, or even visited the site of Ste Marie I, cannot be ascertained. It is reasonable to suppose that they would explore the place for bits of useful European materials, such as metal. Later, visiting Algonkians who came to fish in the Wye would likewise watch for useful goods, and incidentally leave traces of their own possessions. The latter have been found in small quantity.

There is no proof of which the writer is aware that Europeans visited the site between 1649 and 1790, though trappers, traders, missionaries, and explorers may have passed that way without recording the fact. Late in the eighteenth century, British administrators saw the need of opening up the Georgian Bay territory, and to this end made a treaty with the Ojibwa for the purchase of some of their lands. It was entered into by William Claus, superintendent of Indian affairs, at York, in May 22, 1789, with five chieftains of the Ojibwa; as it contains what is probably the first modern reference to Ste Marie I, it deserves to be quoted here: "Beginning at the head or southwesternmost angle of a bay situated above certain French ruins, the head or southwestern-

---

*V. Kinietz, *Indians of the Western Great Lakes* (Ann Arbor, Mich., 1940); D. Jenness, *Indians of Canada* (Ottawa, 1932), pp. 282-3; G. Copway, *Traditional History of the Ojibway Nation* (London, 1850), pp. 86, 91, 95; A. F. Hunter, *A History of Simcoe County* (2 vols., Barrie, 1909), vol. I, p. 10.

most angle of the said bay being called by the Indians Opetikuo-yawsing; thence north 70 degrees to a bay of Lake Huron, called by the Indians Nottaway Sague Bay; thence around the shore to the place of beginning, containing all the land therein, together with the islands in the Harbour of Penetanguishene." And all this for £101 Quebec currency! Further treaties soon brought all of the ancient Huron country under British jurisdiction. But before the treaty-making was completed, the land was being opened up under pressure of war, trade, and settlement. S. Wilmot seems to have made a preliminary survey for the Pene-tanguishene Road in 1811. Seven years later the survey was well under way, and by 1833, it was virtually completed. The Township of Tay, in which the ruins of Ste Marie I are located, was surveyed in 1826 by G. Chewett.

The survey placed the ruins of Ste Marie I in Lot 16, Concession 3, of Tay Township. For a long time it was not known whether they lay in the east or west half of this lot. Actually, however, they are so close to the border line that part of the northwest bastion is in the east half while the main portion is in the west. As we have already seen, Ste Marie I was recognized in 1789 as a "French ruin." Exactly when it was first properly identified would be impossible to say, but Father Chazelle visited it in 1844, apparently fully aware of what it was. Since then, except for a brief interval, its identity has not been questioned.

Title to the west half of Lot 16, and therefore to most of the ruins, was granted in 1829 to one Samuel Richardson; and in 1837, a crown patent bestowed the east half on Pierre Thibeau. The two parts of the site had henceforth, for more than seventy-five years, a complicated history replete with misunderstandings and misconceptions.* The major portion came eventually into the possession of a local sportsman, James Playfair, who left the ruins untouched, but built a hunting lodge, stables, and sheds to the immediate south of them where the Indian compound had stood. He also used large tracts of the adjacent land, including most of the marsh to the south. On his death, the property was

*See *Martyrs' Shrine Message*, vol. VI, no. 4, Dec., 1942, pp. 7, 21.

purchased by the Wye River Hunting Club, and then by Mr. A. W. Taylor of St. Catharines. The Jesuit Fathers bought the site of Ste Marie in 1940, including that part of it owned by Mr. Taylor which lay in the west half, and the few yards of the east half necessary to complete the acquisition of the ruins. Thus did the original mission headquarters, the ancient "Residence," return finally to the possession of its first owners, the Jesuit Order. Since then, in order to round out their holdings adjacent to the historic spot, they have also acquired the large field east and south of the site.

Ste Marie has three hundred years of history behind it—a record exceeded by less than half a dozen settlements in all of North America north of Mexico. Chief among the documents which record it are the *Jesuit Relations*, to which reference has already been made, together with miscellaneous letters and journals by the same authors. A few scattered references to Ste Marie may be found in official reports and other accounts of the period. But one should not overlook the extremely important works of Champlain, of Brother Gabriel Sagard, and of Claude Le Beau, which, while not dealing directly with the site, yet make important contributions to our knowledge of the Indian population which surrounded it and which was the reason for its existence. In later times, the subject has attracted a number of outstanding writers, chief of whom are Francis Parkman and George M. Wrong. Considered as a whole, the early sources supply the student with an array of information scarcely to be rivalled on this continent—an array, incidentally, which is the ethno historian's ideal. They do lack detail, however. The *Jesuit Relations* provide the broad outlines; all facts of primary importance, at least in the narrower historical sense, are there, but the little commonplace developments were not set down. Many reasons come to mind why this should be so; perhaps the authors were too busy to relate them; or perhaps they thought they would not interest their readers; or it may be that they were not interested in such matters as the erection of a new building or the importation of a new cargo of metal tools, deigning them unworthy of being set down alongside the accounts of missionary work. Whatever the cause, such matters usually were omitted.

It is at this point that the archaeologist has been able to make his contribution to the history of the site. By excavation, it has been possible to determine many of the matters pertaining to the physical nature of the settlement upon which the early records are so often silent. Since the buildings were constructed largely of wood, and were burned, it has not been possible for archaeology to assess their height, the number of windows in them, and such details, but it has been possible to determine the ground plan, certain details of the method of construction used, and the types of equipment employed. Though but small additions to knowledge when considered in themselves, yet, taken as a whole, the recovered facts round out the picture, and should make possible the reconstruction of one of Canada's most important historic sites.

DESCRIPTION OF THE SITE

EXPLORATORY WORK AND METHODS OF EXCAVATION

SINCE the time of Father Chazelle, a constant and ever-increasing stream of visitors has come to Ste Marie I. Most important of these, for our purposes, was Father Félix Martin, a Jesuit priest from Montreal. He came in 1855 with a commission from the Canadian Government to explore and excavate the site. Father Martin spent part of the summer of that year at Ste Marie, made numerous water-colour sketches, and excavated part of the ruins. His notes are still unpublished. Through the courtesy of the authorities of St. Mary's College, Montreal, and particularly of Father Lally and Father Desjardins, they have been made available to the writer; extracts from them are appended to this Report. Brief quotations from Father Martin's notes may also be found in Father Jones's *Old Huronia*. No other attempt at excavation was made until the joint enterprise of the Royal Ontario Museum and the Jesuit Order. It should not be forgotten, however, that many people have picked up "curios" there, numerous examples of which have found their way into the collections of the Royal Ontario Museum, and it has been a happy hunting ground for children for a century.

The earliest map of the ruins is apparently one made in 1852 by the Reverend George Hallen, a Church of England clergyman (Map 3). The next appears to have been by Father Martin, who reported that "Our first care was to map out the ground so as to locate the Fort correctly. Once we had cleared away the rubbish which obliterated the lines of the foundations it was an easy matter to trace the outlines and ascertain their dimensions"[*]

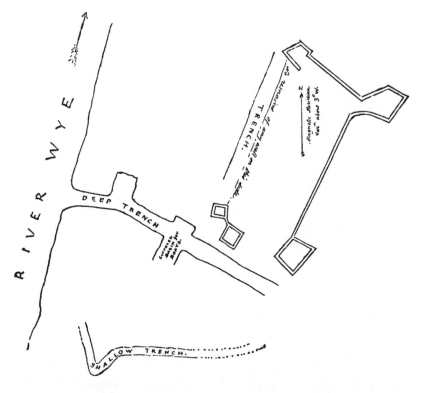

MAP 3. Plan of Ste Marie I, drawn in 1852 by Rev. George Hallen. Reproduced from the *Ontario Archaeological Report*, 1899, p. 59.

(Map 4). The last map of historical importance, reproduced by Hunter on page 14 of his *Report on Huron Village Sites*, was drawn in 1876 by Peter Burnet (Map 5). Both of the published maps have marked similarities.

[*]Jones, *Old Huronia*, p. 10.

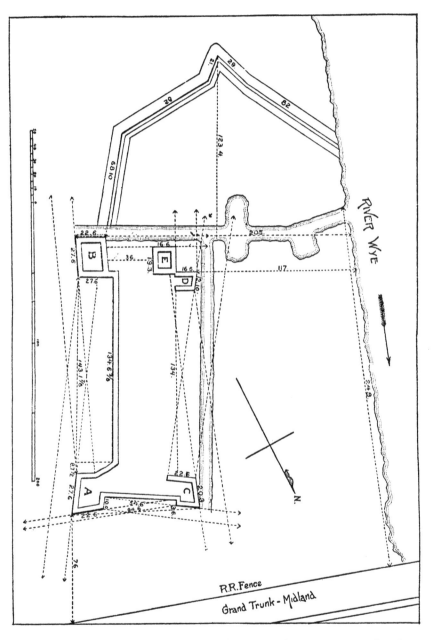

MAP 4. Plan of Ste Marie I, as drawn by Rev. Félix Martin; reproduced from *Old Huronia* by A. E. Jones.

It would be interesting to have full descriptions of the site at various dates. However, scattered observations do exist, and from them we can piece together something of the changing scene. The earliest map, that by Hallen, reveals the moat as the primary feature dividing the site into two halves, the north and the south. The south part has a more or less crescent-shaped redan or "shallow trench" with its maximum distance opposite the east or largest basin. This was the Indian compound. The north part consists of a field and the masonry structures of the Residence or European compound. Hallen's map shows the fort as parallel with the river's bank, and its proportions and orientation are approximately correct. He indicates a trench which appears as wide as the main moat along the west side, and comments that there are "no remains of any wall on this side." He also shows three large bastions at the northwest, northeast, and southeast corners. At the southwest corner, he indicates two small square structures linked by a short wall and with their axes at an angle. The curtains cross the north and south sides without a break. The bastions are not rectangular, but quadrilateral in shape. The northeast bastion is set out from the corner.

Burnet's map is essentially similar, having the two squares in the southeast corner, and the quadrilateral bastions of Hallen's map. However, it shows a break in the east curtain, and some sort of protective wall guarding the portal and its north and east exposures. Moreover, Burnet's main moat is at a considerable angle to the short axis of the fort. He shows the same redan of the Indian compound and the trench along the west side of the Residence, as well as the interior ditch which was still visible in 1940.

These are the meagre details which have come down to us concerning the appearance of the ruin in the nineteenth century. We know that they are inaccurate in some respects, and they may be so in others upon which we have no means of checking; but on the whole, they are tolerably reliable.

Father Martin's water-colour sketches reveal a dense growth of trees, and in his written description, he says that "at present writing the ground is so thickly covered with trees that it is impossible to catch a glimpse of the fort from the landing place,

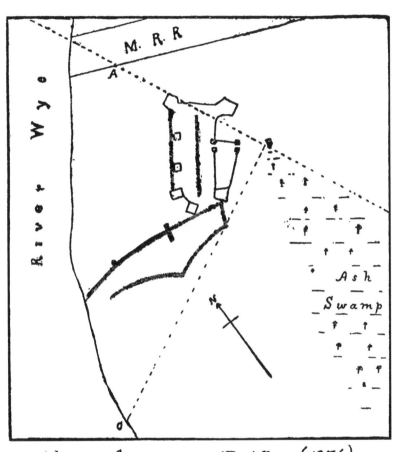

MAP 5. Plan of Ste Marie I, drawn in 1876 by Peter Burnet, public land surveyor; reproduced from the *Ontario Archaeological Report*, 1899, p. 60.

though it is only one hundred and fifty feet from the shore."*
As Sagard bears witness, the country was probably no more
heavily wooded in Huron times than it is today. Changed conditions might have induced a forest growth; at any rate, Burnet's
map shows an "ash swamp" east of the ruins, and if there were
woods to the east, there were probably woods on the site itself.
Martin also refers to the fact that the settlers long remained in
ignorance of "les ruines curieuses, cachées dans l'épaisseure de
leurs forêts."† In pioneer times, most of Ontario was cleared of
forest, at least in the agricultural areas, with the result that large
stretches were virtually treeless for years. The east bank of the
Wye was evidently in this sad condition when the photograph
shown on page 14 of the *Ontario Archaeological Report for 1914*
was taken. No clearing was done on the site after that date. In
fact some of the saplings visible in the cut had grown into large
trees when the excavation began.

In 1885 James Bain, then librarian for the city of Toronto,
reported on the condition of Ste Marie I to the Canadian Institute. He pointed out that, whereas "in 1856 some of the walls
were six feet high," in 1884, "only traces of it [that is, the walls]
were to be found in a few heaps of earth and broken stone."‡

It is remarked in a foot-note in the *Jesuit Relations* that since
"the settlement of the neighborhood, these ruins have undergone great changes."§ David Boyle, commenting in 1891 on Bain's
observations, agreed that "this pretty correctly describes the condition of the ruins to-day, only that things are now a little worse,"
and said that "When I saw it last summer a heavy growth of
weeds covered all that is left of the walls, and rendered it difficult
even to examine the interior, but the outline of structure
including the bastions can still be followed."‖ Eight years later,

---

*F. Martin, *Voyages et recherches*, MS in Archives of St. Mary's College,
Montreal.

†F. Martin, *Autobiographie du père Chaumonot* (Paris, 1885), p. 268. See
also his *Hurons et Iroquois* (Paris, 1882), p. 191, and his *Life of Father Jogues*
(New York, Cincinnati, and St. Louis, 1885), p. 232.

‡J. Bain, "The Present Condition of the Old Fort at Ste Marie" (Canadian
Institute, *Proceedings*, 3rd series, vol. III, 1884-5, p. 278). Father Martin in his
Autobiography of Chaumonot says on p. 58, that in 1854 the ruins still stood to a
height of 1½ meters above ground level.

§*Jesuit Relations*, vol. XIX, p. 270.

‖*Ontario Archaeological Report*, 1890-1, no. 4, p. 18.

the state of affairs seems to have grown still worse, for Hunter observed that "the present condition of the fort scarcely admits of the making of a definite sketch," for it could "be called only a ruin of a ruin."[*] Boyle was of the opinion that this progressive destruction was "not due merely to the ravages of time. Relic hunters have had a considerable share in rasing the works both inside and outside."[†]

In 1893 Harris wrote that the "foundations of this building still remain, and though overgrown with weeds and underbush, may yet be distinctly traced."[‡] It was doubtless the neglected condition of this historic monument that prompted the members of the Canadian Institute to try to purchase the place by public subscription in 1891. Correspondence to this end was carried on, but unavailingly as it turned out.[§] The site continued to deteriorate, though no concerted spoliation took place, probably because the land on which the site stood was not worth the trouble of clearing. Some of the stone, particularly from the northwest bastion, may have been removed, but seemingly little else.

Before excavation was begun, the site presented four large and one small mounds; a low ridge along the north and east sides, a deep hole at the north end, and another one-third the distance up the west side from the moat; a central depression running lengthwise of the ruins near the east side; an open irregular ditch along the west side; the moat and its basins to the south; and a mass of boulders to the north of the southeast bastion (Pl. 1 a, b). A driveway skirted the west side of the ruins, cutting the corner of the northwest mound, and crossing the main moat on a fill. Within 75 feet of the north end passes the Canadian National Railways right of way, running at an angle to the long axis of the fort. Three hundred feet north of the tracks and approximately parallel with them is the concrete highway No. 12. Large quantities of gravel were removed from the area between the

---

[*]*Ontario Archaeological Report,* 1899, p. 59.

[†]*Ibid.,* 1890-1, no. 4, p. 18.

[‡]W. R. Harris, *History of the Early Missions in Western Canada* (Toronto, 1893), p. 90, note.

[§]Canadian Institute, *Transactions, vol. III,* 1891-2; Report of the historical section, p. 59.

tracks and the highway, leaving it low and uneven. North of the
highway is the large hill, the appearance of which has been considerably altered by recent building and grading operations.
Part of it is forested with elm, oak, maple, and, on the lower
slopes, cedar. The dominant growth on the ruins was elm, with
a scattering of hawthorne and Manitoba maple. The largest elm
removed had about seventy annual rings. The treeless area between the ruins and the river bank seemed recently to have been
used as a garden. The grounds around the hunting lodge, which
were once the Indian compound, were now neat lawns, while the
field to the south and east was used as pasturage. This field is
partly marshy. About 500 feet south of the house, the Wye River
is caught by a relatively new concrete dam. Much of this detail
may be seen on the plan shown in Map 6.

The site was carefully surveyed before excavation began. For
this purpose, the Department of Highways for Ontario kindly
loaned the services of Mr. N. D. Bennett and his assistants. Mr.
Bennett's work was extraordinarily complete. He tied in his survey of the site with the provincial highways and topographical
surveys, and made readings to record height above sea-level. He
also prepared a very useful plan of his survey.

The Modified British Grid System was adapted for use on
this site. For this, the selection of a zero point was essential, and
one taken somewhere in the river was considered desirable as
being less subject to change. In considering the direction of the
axes of the survey, moreover, it was felt that since the buildings
of the site had been carefully designed and presumably carefully
placed, it was desirable also to have the axes parallel with some
element in the structures. Accordingly, the east curtain, being
the longest straight line in them and almost parallel with the
river bank, was used. A line two hundred feet west of it was taken
as the north-south axis of the grid, lying as it does in the river's
channel. The zero point of the system was arbitrarily chosen 250
feet south of the main moat, and through it passes the east-west
axis. Consequently, the entire site lies in the northeast quadrant
of the survey, and the European structures in the north part
thereof. The main elements of the buildings and the layout gen-

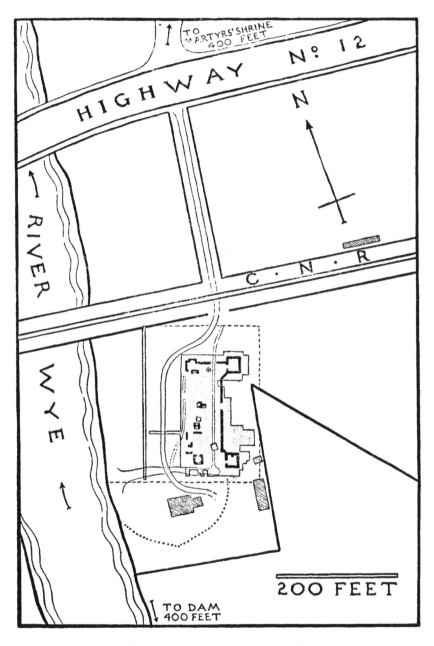

MAP 6. Plan of the site and its environs, as revealed by excavation.

erally correspond very closely in direction to those of the survey, a fact which greatly facilitated the excavation and its description. Should the need ever arise, the system could be expanded indefinitely on either side of the stream.

The north-south axis was divided theoretically into 5-foot intervals, each succeeding 5-foot length being numbered consecutively from one to one hundred; the east-west axis was similarly laid off but named with letters of the alphabet, A, B, C, etc. When it became necessary to repeat, superscript numbers were added thus A^1, B^1, C^1, etc. Lines were produced through these points to cover all the area, dividing it off into 5-foot squares. Reference to these squares is frequently made in the following pages. They were marked from the location in the system as $56C^1$, $87A^2$, etc.* The excavations lie north of the 50-line and east of the M-line (see Map 8).

A bench mark was established at 100U, and consists of a standard iron bar set in concrete. It is correlated with the township survey's bench mark north of the highway on Shrine property, and its height above sea-level established with reference to the same point. All bearings, as Mr. Bennett observes in a footnote to his map, "are referred to the astronomic meridian through the southeasterly angle of the E½ of Lot 16, Con. IV of the Township of Tay, as shown on Deposited Plan No. 16364." Contours are shown on the detail map at 0.5-foot intervals, at every 5-foot stake on the ruins, and at every 10-foot stake on the remainder of the site.

While the survey was being made, trees which were likely to be in the way later were cut down and removed, poison ivy was eradicated, and the site generally cleaned up. Stumps remained until the feature upon which each stood was excavated; they were then removed by chopping and chiselling. They could only be taken out at the expense of much time and labour, but nevertheless, surprisingly little damage to the site resulted from their removal.

*On the Department of Highways contour map, all the letters of the alphabet were used, but on field maps, "I" was dropped to avoid confusion with "J": all spatial references occurring in this Report are based on this modification.

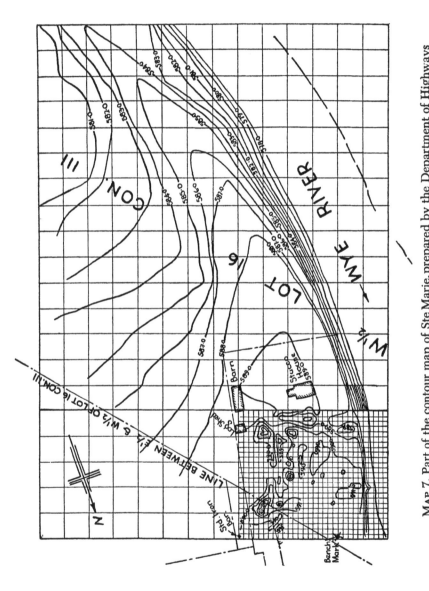

MAP 7. Part of the contour map of Ste Marie, prepared by the Department of Highways previous to excavation.

A careful surface examination resulted in the finding of nothing more than a quantity of modern material such as nails, bones, tin cans, and the like.

The areal unit of excavation throughout was the 5-foot square, each with its own designation. Vertically, the unit was a 3-inch level; that is to say, excavation proceeded by removing 3 inches of material uniformly over the surface of a unit area 5 feet square, then advancing to the next level. Shovels, trowels, grape-fruit knives, paint brushes, and camel's hair brushes were the tools, with sieves used as circumstances required. Dirt was wheeled away in barrows and dumped well beyond the excavation. Graphs were drawn of all significant soil features, and profile drawings made of the sides of trenches to show stratification and so forth. Photographs of soil features, of specimens *in situ,* and of all-over views were taken as work progressed, scale diagrams were made of important structures, and ground plans were sketched as they were revealed. Elevation readings were frequently taken, particularly on soil strata and on significant structures, and even specimens *in situ.*

During the first season's work each square was excavated to undisturbed soil before the next was touched. This procedure had the advantage of giving full knowledge of the specimens in the particular square under investigation, and much detail concerning its structure, especially its profile. It led, however, to certain difficulties in interpretation, since it meant the obliteration, for instance, of the floor, square by square, and the consequent difficulty of getting a clear conception of the larger area. After the first season, therefore, the exhaustive excavation of squares was abandoned in favour of clearing, level by level, as large an area as might be desired. All descriptions were still given in terms of square designations. The revised method was used in excavating the Chapel floor; it was exposed as a unit, though when necessary it was still possible to excavate deeper in a given square to trace down exceptional features such as the deep hollow in front of the central fireplace. The modification seemed to suit the exigencies of the site better than the original method, and yet no material information was lost.

Specimens were collected by square and level, were studied,

cleaned, and repaired where necessary, and were then segregated as to material (bone, metal, pottery, etc.), given a catalogue number, bagged, and stored. The catalogue system was designed to indicate by numbers used the site where found, the square, the level, and the sequence number of the bag. Frequently several specimens of the same material from the same square and level are included in the same bag and bear the same number.*

Perhaps it should be explained here that all specimens which it was thought might later prove helpful in studying the site were saved. This involved the collecting and bagging, for instance, not only of relatively uncommon things like potsherds, bone, and glass, but also of an unexpected and very large amount of charcoal and brick-like material. There was indeed so much of this that only large or especially useful specimens were kept.

Excavation of Ste Marie I was decided upon in the spring of 1941, and by the end of June the field party was on the site. It was agreed that the Royal Ontario Museum should supply the necessary technical assistance and what equipment it possessed; and that the Jesuit Order would provide accommodation for the staff and any additional assistance which might be required. The Museum was to receive the right to all scientific data, and the Order all specimens unless otherwise decided upon.

There were four members in the Museum party. From time to time, volunteer workers joined the staff and lent valuable aid. The Jesuit Order supplied during the first season the services of six day-labourers, all elderly French-speaking Canadians from nearby villages, and during the succeeding season, four or five as circumstances permitted. Help became difficult to obtain, especially after the first summer, and even more difficult to keep because of the increasing labour shortage in industry. Under the circumstances, it was almost out of the question to hope to train helpers, or to have any degree of continuity in them. The Order

*In numbering specimens, the following system was employed. The site was designated by the signature S. Following S appears the number of the level in which the specimen was found, for example, S12. The square number follows, as 71 Q^2. Finally, the bag number is added. Thus the number appears as S12. 71Q^1. 2, etc.

did everything in its power to get auxiliary help, even to drawing upon its regular ground staff; it also made its trucks and other facilities available for exceptional jobs, and contributed wheelbarrows, packing boxes, cartons, etc. At the end of the first season, the Order generously erected a small workshop for the use of the field staff where sorting, numbering, and cataloguing were subsequently done, and specimens and equipment stored.

In the course of the excavation, a test trench was run from the south side of the moat along the U-line to 99U in the open field between the fort and the river. It is conveniently referred to as the U-Trench. At right angles to this, along the 66-line, another test trench was cut, starting at the river and crossing the entire ruins to end in 66F². It is known as the 66-Trench. A few squares were omitted in both trenches where the soil was obviously never disturbed. Test pits, usually half squares, were sunk in various other parts of the site, seven of them in the area once occupied by the Indian compound. A third test trench was dug east of the European structure along the H¹-line. The European compound was completely excavated to depths varying from 6 inches to several feet, and the ground adjacent to it for a width of 10 feet was similarly studied.

A total of 20,000 square feet was uncovered, and 29,961 cubic feet, or 1,109 cubic yards of dirt were removed. Stone recovered from the European compound amounted to 6,626 cubic feet. Over 40,000 specimens were collected, but this number includes many pieces of material which, strictly speaking, do not deserve to be listed individually, such as charcoal, samples of mortar, and small bits of scrap metal and bones. It is obviously next to impossible to say when a specimen should be counted individually and when similar things should be lumped with it and the collection counted as one. Catalogue entries number 8,080.

II. The Excavation

EXPLORATORY WORK

(a) The U-Trench

THE necessary exploratory work was begun in the open space between the river and the ruins proper. It should be remarked here, however, that no attempt was made to make an independent study of this area; it was examined only in so far as it related to the main structures, for it was no part of the undertaking to excavate it thoroughly.* This little field presumably may have served at various times as a garden, and again as building space for temporary structures. At any rate, it seemed unlikely to be of major importance, and appeared to be a suitable place in which to begin preliminary work.

Exploration began at the north end of the line marked U on the diagrams—henceforth called the U-Trench—and continued southward to the south side of the main moat, ending with 51U. Alternate squares only were opened at the northern extremity because the soil appeared to be undisturbed below the plough line (7 to 9 inches). From 68U southwards, however, all squares were opened, as evidence of disturbance became abundant (Pl. II a).

Square 99U exemplified the soil structure of the site admirably. The top soil was a mixture of humus and sand about 7 to 9 inches deep. Below this lay 6 inches of sand, slightly reddish-brown in colour, with rusty blotches. Below this again was varved clay, blue when wet, but drying to a whitish or greyish colour. It was exceedingly sticky and unpleasant to work when wet. The varves were generally thin (¼ to 1 inch) and the formation of indeterminate depth (Fig. 1).

In view of the ploughing to which it had been subjected, it is not surprising that both ancient and modern materials were found in the top soil. Occasionally, modern specimens were found much

---

*This area has since been excavated by the University of Western Ontario, under the supervision of Mr. Wilfrid Jury, and the work is, at writing, nearing completion.

lower, for instance, in 54U where there had been a recent fill. Usually, however, ancient specimens were found in the lower levels and modern ones at or near the surface. On the other hand, a small medal probably cast prior to 1622 in honour of Ignatius Loyola and Francis Xavier was found in the topsoil, so not all ancient material was deeply buried.

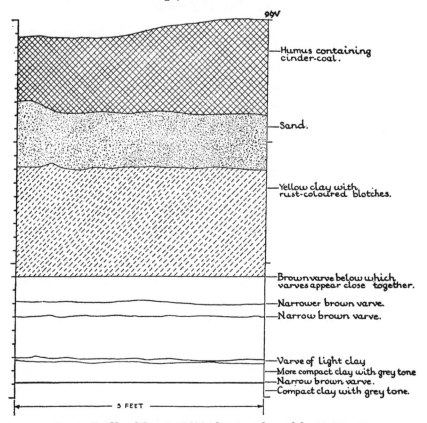

FIG. 1. Profile of Square 99U, showing the soil formation at Ste Marie I.

The first eighteen squares opened revealed nothing except occasional post-moulds which proved to be modern. South of 67U two open-air hearths or camp-fires came to light. The first was a small, rectangular bed of ash which disappeared at a depth of 1 foot. It yielded a quantity of Indian material, such as two pieces of chert, a piece of mauve clay pigment, fifty fragments of bird and fish bone, as well as a quantity of charcoal and a red glass bead. Its most conspicuous product was a small brass button embossed on the face with a circle of small fleur-de-lis and crosses. Another hearth in 63U was larger and more productive. It had originally been a concave pit, 3 feet wide and 30 inches deep, but successive fires had filled it up with ash, charcoal, and débris. A number of cracked fieldstones, mostly small, and more abundant near the edge, indicated the use of hot stones for boiling water. A few pieces of bird bone came from the lowest level; level 7 yielded an iron hook, probably a fish-hook, and the level above more bones. A clam shell, and some bird and fish bones lay in level 4 with a piece of red ochre, and just below the humus line was a fragmentary clay pipe bowl made in the shape of a human head with face toward the smoker and wearing a small round cap (Fig. 27, K).

(b) The 66-Trench

While this trench crossed the site from west to east, only those sections not actually in the ruins are described here, as they are the exploratory portions; the others are included in the description of the excavation of the compound.

As the trench was driven eastward, evidence of disturbance in the soil itself and in the specimens rapidly increased. Limestone nodules and chips became more abundant as the compound was approached. A count of these was maintained, but revealed nothing of significance other than the rapidity with which they increased toward the east, as many as 450 lying in level 7 of square 66Z. An Indian hearth also existed in this square. It extended into level 10, had a diameter of 5 feet (in level 5), and revealed many limestone chips around its sides. Its contents consisted of dark ash and charcoal principally, with some patches of clay and a few specimens such as a chert scraper and an iron trade axe.

In 66B, an unusual structure was excavated, which later was seen to extend a square to the east and the same distance to the south. A strip of hard-packed clay 3 feet wide lay in a north-south direction, and an eastward and westward extension apparent at the north gave it a cruciform shape. The edges were bordered on the west by a 2-foot-wide strip of pure ash and on the east by a band of lime, while at the north end was a circular patch of pure lime. The abundance of this material makes it nearly certain that here was the lime-kiln or mixing trough used in building the fort.

Excavation in the trench revealed a number of benches of hard clay in sand, as well as post-moulds. No significance seemed to attach to the patches; the post-moulds may possibly have had some connection with the fort.

The specimens discovered in the humus included quantities of bird and animal bones, a lead ball, ancient and modern nails, a few pieces of glass, a piece of green-glaze pottery, several fragments of brick-like material (some of it fused), a few lumps of coal, lead, and other modern refuse. The most conspicuous item recovered from the surface layer was the above-mentioned oval medallion of bronze or silver, bearing the likenesses of Loyola and Francis Xavier, which was found in 67B (Fig. 23, A). Specimens of seventeenth-century French origin included two blue glass beads and a trade axe, as well as quantities of mortar and brick-like material. A clay pipe stem with a spiral decoration, ochre and chert, and a fragmentary black clay pipe bowl are all of Indian origin.

(c) The 63-Trench

In a trench beginning at the west edge of the field and cut towards the east along the 63-line, soil conditions and specimens similar to those uncovered in the 66- and U-Trenches were revealed. A band of dark soil, however, was first noticed in 67R and continued eastward in a straight line to the fort. It was about 1 foot wide, and extended down for a distance of 2 feet. The fill in this band was hard-packed clay embedded with bits of mortar and small fragments of limestone. Post-moulds were found close to it in places and in 63F another fill of the same sort intersected it at right angles. Such features were encountered elsewhere on the site, seemingly making a pattern of their own—which will be described in another connection (pp. 87-8).

(d) Other Preliminary Work

Exploratory work in other areas revealed virtually nothing of importance. To the east of the compound, there was some surface disturbance; but nothing in the way of material except a few modern bones. Test trenches in the vicinity of the sheds—where the Indian compound once was—showed no disturbance and yielded no specimens.

(e) Evidence from Exploratory Work

The evidence gleaned from the exploratory work indicates that the field between the compound and the river was used by both Europeans and Indians, probably contemporaneously. The medallion, scraps of metal, mortar, and other remains bear evidence of its use by the French. Indians probably disturbed the area further by digging holes in various places for their hearths. Since both Indian artifacts and trade goods are found in them, they post-date the coming of Europeans. The pipe fragment was certainly Huron and as Sagard mentions the use of paints by these people, we may be sure the clay pigment was also theirs.[*] There is nothing of Indian origin that can be attributed to any tribe but the Hurons; hence the age of the hearths and their contents must be similar to that of the fort and they must be of Huron construction. It is quite possible, though difficult to prove, that the hearths date from the year 1649, for Huron Indians probably came to the site to camp until they departed for Christian Island. It is unlikely that the Jesuits would want them to use the field in earlier times, especially if the missionaries themselves used it for a garden.

Evidence of disturbance in other trial diggings was negative. As for the north end of the field near the river, this may mean nothing more than that the spot was either used as a garden or completely neglected. So far as the area south of the European compound was concerned, there is historical evidence that it was disturbed, having been set aside for Indian use with appropriate buildings. In this case, the negative evidence can only mean that testing was not extensive enough. The same stricture may be applicable to the work east of the European compound, for we know that somewhere near by, and very probably in the area just mentioned, there was a cemetery with a number of interments.

[*]Br. Gabriel Sagard-Théodat, Le Grand Voyage au pays des Hurons (Paris, n.d.), pp. 135, 154, 155. F. G. Bressani, Relation . . . de la Nouvelle France (Montreal, 1852) also mentions it.

The labour and expense of exploring such large areas where the possibilities of securing evidence were so small were felt to be unwarranted at the time.

EXCAVATION OF THE COMPOUND

The excavation of the European compound and its accessory structures occupied the greater amount of time and yielded the major portion of interesting results and specimens. In addition to uncovering the four bastions and the two curtain walls, which could be dimly discerned even before work began, the excavation brought to light two major buildings which had been burned to the ground, namely, the Residence and the Chapel, as well as indications of a workshop, sentry walks, and the remains of a storage pit and short pieces of wall. Most of these are of the highest significance in so far as reconstruction is concerned. Their placement, dimensions, and many minor details were recorded, and something learned of their function and relationships. These details will be treated systematically in the following pages dealing with the structures.

It may be of interest, however, to give at this point some idea of the size of the compound and the placement of its elements. The maximum length from north to south, i.e. along the east side, amounts to 182 feet; and the greatest width from east to west is at the north end, where the distance is 94 feet. There existed a bastion at each of the four corners, although at the southwest corner a second structure appears on early plans farther to the west than the one still remaining. The east and north sides of the compound were protected by low curtains of stone, probably in Jesuit times supplied with wooden superstructures. No defensive work was found along the south except the moat. The west walls of Residence and Chapel, apparently without doors, provided sufficient security in that direction, except for the space between the south end of the Residence and the bastion which was left unprotected, unless a fragmentary piece of very poor masonry wall is accepted as evidence to the contrary.

Ten feet north of the southwest bastion the foundations of a forge flue indicate that here was the workshop for the establish-

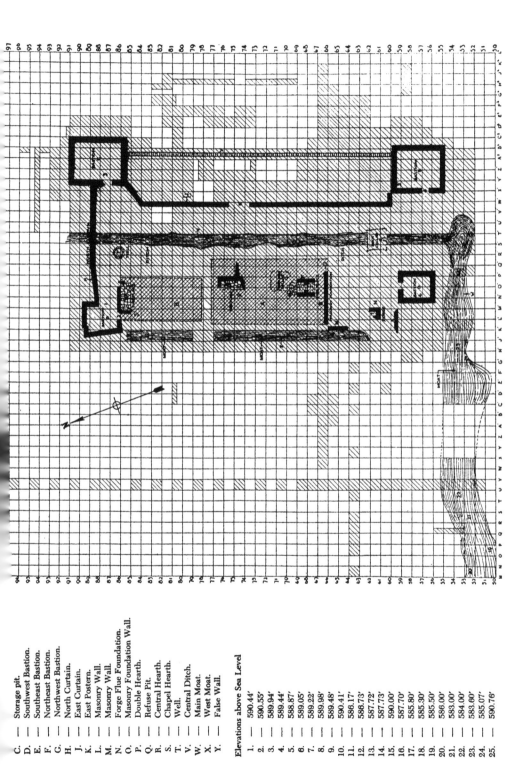

C. — Storage pit.
D. — Southwest Bastion.
E. — Southeast Bastion.
F. — Northeast Bastion.
G. — Northwest Bastion.
H. — North Curtain.
J. — East Curtain.
K. — East Postern.
L. — Masonry Wall.
M. — Masonry Wall.
N. — Forge Flue Foundation.
O. — Masonry Foundation Wall.
P. — Double Hearth.
Q. — Refuse Pit.
R. — Central Hearth.
S. — Chapel Hearth.
T. — Well.
V. — Central Ditch.
W. — Main Moat.
X. — West Moat.
Y. — False Wall.

Elevations above Sea Level

1. — 590.44'
2. — 590.55'
3. — 589.94'
4. — 589.44'
5. — 588.87'
6. — 589.05'
7. — 589.22'
8. — 589.98'
9. — 589.48'
10. — 590.41'
11. — 586.17'
12. — 586.73'
13. — 587.72'
14. — 587.73'
15. — 590.00'
16. — 587.70'
17. — 585.80'
18. — 585.30'
19. — 585.50'
20. — 586.00'
21. — 583.00'
22. — 584.00'
23. — 583.60'
24. — 585.07'
25. — 590.76'

Map. 8. Plan of the excavations, showing the arrangement of buildings and other features.

ment, and the abundance of scrap and waste material provides additional confirmation. Thirty-five feet north of the same bastion stood the south wall of the Residence, which was itself 56 feet long from north to south. Immediately north of the Residence, and so placed that their west walls were in line, was the structure which appears to have been the Chapel. This building was contiguous to the northwest bastion. About 10 feet east of the north end of the Chapel, and within the fortification walls, was a well which appears to date from Jesuit times. At the south end again, about 8 feet north of the southwest bastion and 10 west of the east curtain, an underground chamber was discovered, which appears to have been used as a storage cellar for vegetables and foods, and probably at a later time for refuse.

In addition to the structures, this area also yielded large numbers of artifacts, both European and Indian.

(a) The Residence

The Residence proper, the building in which the Fathers, brothers, labourers, soldiers, and others attached to the establishment actually lived, is believed to have stood along the west side of the compound, and nearly at its centre. The evidence for this is a wooden sill, a masonry foundation wall, two large fireplaces, wooden flooring, and a kind of refuse pit beneath part of that flooring. The area covered by this structure also yielded more specimens than any other with the single exception of the workshop site. The Residence was the largest single building at Ste Marie; it was probably two storeys high, included both masonry and wooden construction, and in many ways must have presented an appearance of some comfort and completeness. On its north, and probably contiguous to it, stood the Chapel; a short distance south, the workshop; to the east, an open space bounded by the walls of the fort; while on the west (the river side) the walls of Residence and Chapel afforded in themselves a sufficient protection (Map 8, A).

On the south, the limits of the Residence were marked by the presence of the masonry foundation (Fig. 2). This appeared at Level 3, or 9 inches below the surface. When fully exposed it was seen to extend from 3 feet east of 66L^1 to 2.6 feet east of 66P^1, a distance of 19.6 feet, and to have a width of 1.6 feet. Built of cut limestone, most of which was in the form of small slabs laid in mortar, it was slightly enlarged at each end, probably for added strength (Map 8, O).

The position of the west wall of the Residence was clearly marked by the charred sill which was found in position (Fig. 3 and Pl. III *a*). Even in its fragmentary condition, this was well enough preserved to yield a considerable amount of information. It was originally a stout timber, some 15 inches in diameter and wider than it was deep. The upper surface was hollowed out to make a concave trough 5 inches wide and the same depth. Exact dimen-

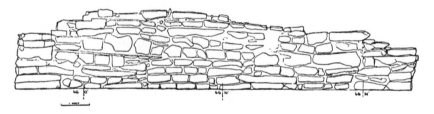

Fig. 2. Foundation wall of the Residence, in side view.

sions are extremely hard to determine in such fragile material, and may not accurately indicate the original size, but are likely a reasonably close approximation to it. The ends of two stakes or upright timbers which had been wedged into this sill were found in position, a fact which suggests that a continuous row of such stakes constituted the outside wall of the Residence and, as we shall see later, of the Chapel. The stakes were doubtless fitted at the top into another large timber corresponding to the sill at the bottom.[*] The sill itself appears to have been spliced in square 70L[1]; for six large angle-irons, L-shaped, and each about 7 inches long, were placed so that the short arm at the top was driven into the timber near its upper edge; when found, the long ends were resting in the soil. Such clamps apparently were used to keep the spliced sections from shifting.

The line of the sill deviates somewhat from that of the east curtain; the north end being a little more than 1 ½ feet west of the

[*]See Marius Barbeau, "The House that Mac Built" (*Beaver*, outfit 276, Dec., 1945, pp. 10-13), in which this type of construction is well described.

south end. Sills of Residence and Chapel, moreover, seemed not to be continuous, though in line, for there was an interruption of about 2 ½ feet in 77L¹. The total determined length of the sill in this structure is 56 feet.

As for the limits of the Residence on the north, no positive evidence can be presented. It is, however, clear that the south wall of the Chapel lay along the 78-line, ending on the east at 78P¹. No similar evidence exists for a wall to the Residence. There was an interruption, it will be recalled, in the sill in Square 77L¹, which

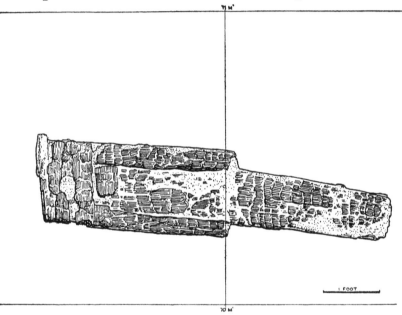

FIG. 3. Fragment of charred wood from sill in the Residence.

would suggest that an east-west sill probably extended eastward beginning in that square. Instead, a zone about 3 feet wide along the south side of the Chapel wall yielded relatively few specimens, but unusually large quantities of burnt clay or daub. It may be that a mud wall existed here, and has since crumbled away. If so, it is still difficult to establish the eastern limit of this wall. Two possibilities present themselves. First, in view of the fact that the Chapel wall ends at 78P¹, and the outside of the chimney wall is in line with this, it is possible that the east wall of the Residence also lay close to the P¹-line. Secondly, the north wall may have continued farther east than this, as suggested in the evidence below for the position of the east wall.

Wooden flooring covered parts of squares 74P¹ and 74Q¹ and even in 75Q¹ and 75R¹ there were boards which suggested flooring. Hence the eastern wall may possibly have begun 2 ½ feet east of 66Q¹ and continued north along that line, past the refuse pit. This would account for the existence of the flooring at the southeast corner of the fireplace; but the evidence is obviously inconclusive.

Charred wooden flooring was evident in various sections of the building, notably in the southwest corner, along the west side, and at the north end. In those sections where no floor remained, it is assumed that the wood, which was never burned, rotted away. No board was intact for all of its original length, though some were still 3 or 4 feet long. A dozen or more were carefully measured and their widths found to range from 5 to 21 inches, but more commonly they were 7, 8, 9, and 10 inches, and their thicknesses from 1½ to 3 inches. From this it is obvious that floor boards were hand hewn, probably with the very axes and the adze found elsewhere on the site.

A study of Map 9 will reveal that, while most of the floor boards ran east and west, there were some which lay north and south. In one or two places indeed there are two floors, one laid on top of the other; in these cases the earlier floor has the north-south placement.

The largest and best-preserved section of flooring lay between the west sill and the great fireplace at the north end. It covered a considerable area southwest of the fireplace with a few boards north of it and a large section southeast of it. The evidence for flooring northeast of the structure and at the north edge of the refuse pit was unsatisfactory. The chinks in the floor may have been rather numerous, for many small specimens were found beneath the boards. Not everything was thus lost, by any means, for on top of the floor lay such noteworthy articles as part of an ivory rosary and several axes. In one place, part of a meal was evidently spilled, for beans and corn were found. The floors were generally lower than the hearths; in the case of the double fireplace the difference in level amounted to 5 inches.

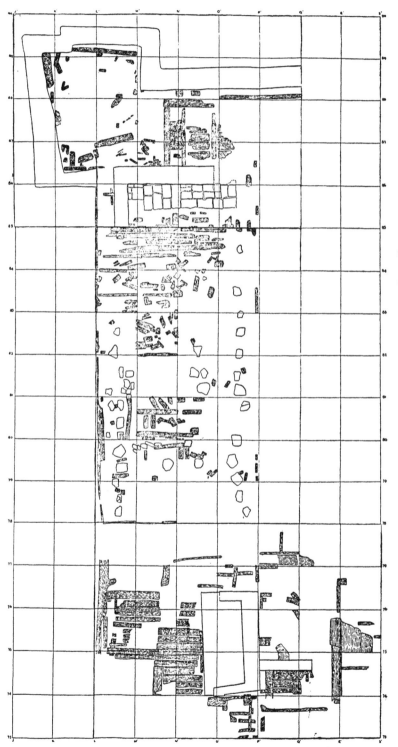

MAP 9. Plan of portion of the excavated area to show flooring.

SCALE - 1 SQ. - 5 FEET

Supporting timbers, some of which resembled modern scantlings, were of several sizes and shapes. Two large, hollowed-out timbers abutted on the sill and extended eastward towards the refuse pit; one of them was in 72L[1] and the other in 70L[1] - 70M[1]. The larger was 4 ½ feet long and 2 ½ wide, and appeared to be one log hollowed out. The ends of two uprights remained in the channel. The placement of the feature indicates that a partition stood here. The other timber was 9 feet long and 2 ½ wide, also hollowed out. The channel was shallow, nearly as wide as the timber, and retained no upright posts. Remains of a heavy upright timber were present in a squared recess left in the west wall of the double fireplace, which may have served as a roof support. The recess was in the middle of the wall, so that it was in line with the chimney wall. A similar timber, though much smaller, was placed in the outer southwest corner of the great fireplace wall. Small timbers were evident in various places, particularly round about the great fireplace and south of it. Most of them had almost certainly been floor joists. Those north of the fireplace showed no systematic arrangement, however, and had probably fallen from above.

THE DOUBLE FIREPLACE

One of the most interesting and unusual architectural features was the fireplace with two hearths, one of which was extended to make a small paved area. There was little of the structure left, a few of the lower courses only, but enough remained to indicate that there had been a dividing wall between the hearths, above which they shared a common flue (Map 8,P and Pl. xvii, b). The structure was situated 5 ½ feet north of the masonry wall described above. As nearly as it could be measured, in its disintegrated condition, it was 7 ½ feet wide on the south, 8 ¼ on the north, and 7 ¼ at both sides in the other dimension. This practically square unit was divided near the centre by the wall which separates the hearth in an E-W direction. Like other carefully made masonry, it is of cut limestone and limestone flags, laid in mortar (Fig. 4).

The foundation walls along the east and west ends were 1 foot wide, and the dividing wall 1 ½ feet; all showed the usual hearting of small stones. The east wall was followed to its foundation, which extended 1¾ feet below hearth level; the lower portions were either not so well built or they had sagged considerably since being laid. There was no footing. In a niche on the outside of the west wall, opposite to the dividing wall, was the charred remains of an upright post which had helped to carry the upper

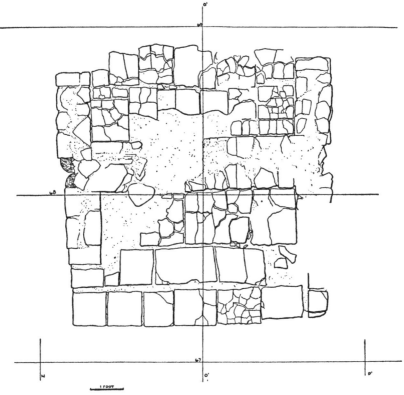

Fig. 4. Plan of double hearth.

structure of the building. A corresponding niche seemed to have existed in the east wall, but since that element had been so severely damaged by the roots of a large tree, its existence cannot be definitely asserted. The side walls did not extend the full width of the hearths; for instance, they stopped 15 inches short of the edge of the south hearth.

The care with which the flags had been dressed and the neatness of their placing combined to give the hearths a most attractive appearance notwithstanding the fact that no special support had been given to them. Most of the stones suffered extreme damage from heat, frost, and moisture, and consequently were fractured and cracked into small sections. Originally they were about a foot square, although some in the north hearth were as much as 1¾ feet by 1½ feet. Several were missing when the structure was exposed.

As noted, the flagging of the north hearth extended a considerable distance beyond the side walls, to form a sort of pavement, but how far it went is not known. It seems to have stretched at least 3 feet north and covered part of the refuse pit.

The débris on the hearth floors contained a great quantity of ash and charcoal (some of it from hardwood), burnt bones, and metal goods. Amongst the latter were numerous nails, some iron spikes, an axe, and a piece of copper. Beneath the edge of the floor at the south side two metal pins were found, modern in shape but undoubtedly of seventeenth-century origin (Pl. XLI, G, H).

This double fireplace must have been an important feature of the establishment. To judge from its placement, it was used more for such utilitarian purposes as cooking, than for ornamental or social ones. Very probably it was situated between refectory and pantry or bakehouse, where one hearth could be used for routine cooking and baking, and the other for both heating the dining hall and for roasting. The areas south and west are known to have been floored, and it seems likely that flooring existed northward also.

Not enough stone was found on the location to reconstruct the fireplace, which would necessarily be of stone construction, even to the height of 10 or 12 feet, much less to a height of 25 or 30 feet. Therefore at least some stone was removed subsequent to the destruction of the fort. The upper parts may possibly have been built of wood heavily coated on the inside with mud. In the event that above the 10 or 12-foot level wood was used, the amount of stone would be proportionately less, and to this the scarcity of stone may in part be due.

REFUSE PIT

The refuse pit, situated immediately north of the double fireplace was a bowl-shaped depression. The roof had collapsed, the

contours had become rounded, and in the bottom of the con-
cavity a large elm tree was growing. Another elm growing on
the edge of the hearth had damaged the flagging which once had
extended out to cover part of the pit. Much of the flagging had
slid down into the depression (Map 8, Q).

Excavation of this feature was carried out near the end of
the second season's work, at a time when heavy rains kept it almost
constantly flooded. What with fallen boulders, tree roots, and
water it proved a difficult task indeed, and it was virtually impossible to make accurate measurements.

The surface consisted of humus beneath which lay sand or
brick. Burnt clay was particularly abundant north of the fireplace, forming in some places a solid bed as much as 1 foot deep.
Beneath the top layers, the soil was markedly stratified, indicating
a fill. The profile on the south wall of the pit may be taken as
typical. It shows, beneath the burnt clay material, a layer of
charcoal—probably from an old flooring. Under this was a band,
6 to 8 inches wide, consisting of a mixture of clay, humus, and
sand, and containing also some charcoal and a few fragments of
burnt clay. Then followed another thin band of humus impreg-
nated with charcoal, pure humus, and finally sand. This alterna-
tion of humus and sand could be followed in most parts of the pit,
suggesting that refuse had been thrown in and covered from time
to time with sand. At least two distinct bands of vegetable
matter, one of which was on the floor of the pit, could be seen
distinctly. They contained seeds similar to those found in the
floor of the storage pit, later to be described. A few artifacts were
found, but less than one might expect from a general refuse pit,
which fact suggests that it was used only for organic waste. There
were, however, a few iron nails, a corner from a rectangular glass
bottle, some bone and burnt bone, and in level 8 one or two
pieces of worked chert and a few scraps of iron.

Posts first appeared in level 9, that is, about 2¼ feet below the
general level, and when exposed were seen to be arranged approximately in a square, 8½ feet in E-W width and 9 feet in N-S
length. Fifty-eight posts made up the stockade, each of them
sharpened at the lower end with an iron axe, and driven into the
clay subsoil so that they sloped outward slightly. They were made

of lengths of small cedar tree trunks which had been roughly chopped to the proper length, with the bark still on in most cases, and sharpened at one end. The lower portions were remarkably well preserved, the cut surfaces being almost as fresh as when made. Axe notches can be seen on the upper ends of at least three stakes, although the tops had generally suffered some decay. The tallest stake measured 4½ feet, the shortest 2¾, while the average

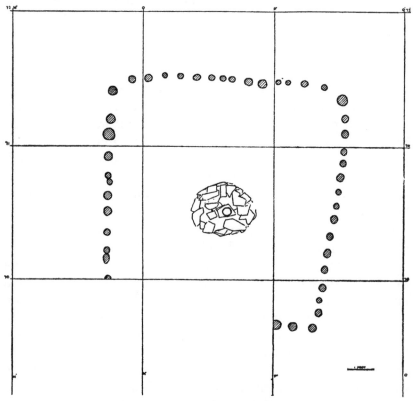

FIG. 5. Plan of the refuse pit.

was 4 feet. In circumference they ranged from 7 to 16 inches. Corner stakes were only slightly larger than the others (Fig. 5, Pl. vi *a*).

A stick 22 inches long protruded at an angle from a small group of stones near the centre of the pit floor. Presumably it had once been longer and supported the ceiling. The bottom of the pit, which was nearly flat, lay about 6 feet below the general level of the surface. Along the east side, fragments, partly of charred and partly of decayed timber, were found 1½ feet below the surface: one piece appeared to have been hollowed out on its upper surface.

The structure may be summarized as an almost square pit about 6 feet deep and 9 feet across, whose clay walls were retained by driven stakes of cedar, and whose roof appears to have been supported by a small post. Organic material thrown in was covered from time to time with a layer of sand.

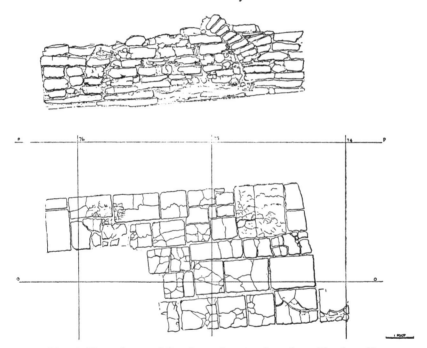

FIG. 6. Plan of central fireplace, showing hearth and back-wall.

THE GREAT FIREPLACE

The largest fireplace on the site was situated in the northeast corner of the Residence (Map 8, R). It had a single large hearth, facing west, and a short piece of masonry wall projecting eastwards at right angles to the chimney wall and 1¾ feet north of the southeast corner. The complex was one of the best preserved structures on the site; 3 feet of chimney wall were still standing above the hearth floor in 1941 (Fig. 6, Pls. vii a, xix a).

A large and irregular mound of dirt, rubble, and stone was all that could be seen before excavation. Because of its elevation above the general level, the spot had been selected as a suitable place for the erection of a monument to the memory of the martyrs Brébeuf and Lalemant. These men were killed at St. Ignace, brought to Ste Marie, buried for a short period, and later exhumed, their larger bones being taken away by the departing Jesuits. The granite monolith is therefore not a grave marker as many suppose, but a memorial stone only. Its presence, however, made the mound even more conspicuous than nature had done and serves to identify it in many photographs of the site. In addition, two stout elms grew on the mound's eastern slope, their powerful roots firmly gripping the remains of the chimney wall. Enough humus accumulated on the surface to support a scanty growth of grass and weeds (Pls. iv *b*, vi *b*).

The débris was carefully cleared away, the stone piled by itself, and the feature excavated as far as possible in a unit. When excavation was complete it was seen that the lower parts of the chimney and side walls were more or less intact, that the upper part of the chimney had collapsed to the west, that the hearth was tolerably well preserved, that the lower part of the eastward-extending wall was intact, and that the structure was surrounded by a wooden flooring, except perhaps on the north and east. A deep layer of grey ash on the hearth had both charred and un-charred bones embedded in it; above this was a mixture of charred wood and ash, indicating a collapsed ceiling or roof, and above this again a deep layer of stone and mortar. Around the outside of the structure on the east and south, and more especially in the southeast exterior corner, was a deep deposit of burnt clay, topped with stones and mortar; it contained virtually no specimens except a few pieces of brick. Close to the exterior of the south wall at floor level were the broken and partly burned remains of an antler ladle (Fig. 31, B).

The accessory east-west wall may properly be described first, since it seems to be merely an appendage to the fireplace. Its function, unless to support the chimney wall, or to close the north side of the Residence at that spot, is unknown. It was built of well-fashioned, rectangular limestone blocks varying considerably in size, and laid in courses of mortar. At the west end its thickness was 21 inches but it narrows to 14 inches at the east. The length was 7 feet; the eastern end is badly disintegrated. There was a narrow footing.

The chimney wall in over-all measurement was 11¾ feet long from north to south, and a trifle more than 2 feet thick. It was placed at a slight angle to the grid, and therefore to the main axis of the compound, the north end being farther west than the south. In construction, the element was like the bastion walls; that is, cut limestone blocks were laid in courses in mortar with hearting of small stones or chips. The outer faces of the blocks were squared, but the inner were left rough to increase their bonding qualities. The outer face of the wall presented a pleasing appearance even though it had suffered damage from the tree roots. A small recess where one block had been omitted existed near the south side, but north of the accessory wall. If it was functional, its use is unknown (Pl. xix b).

The inner face presented a different appearance. The lower courses consisted of long, thin slabs. Above these, the stones in the courses were so arranged that some of them formed a narrow arch. The arch began 1½ feet from each end of the hearth, and appeared to have had an original height of slightly more than 3 feet, although its upper part was destroyed. The portion of the chimney wall enclosed by the arch differed from the rest only in being less regularly coursed, and in being composed of somewhat smaller stones. The stones in the arch were generally flatter than those in the wall. Plate iv b shows the general effect of the construction. Despite the fact that the arch added to the beauty of the structure, it appeared to have been concealed under a coat of plaster. The intense heat of numerous fires and subsequent exposure to moisture and frost had destroyed nearly all the plaster and cracked most of the stones into small fragments. The lower and more central portions had been most severely damaged in this way.

Of the north side wall 5 feet remained. It was at a right angle to the back wall, and where the two join was 2½ feet high. Its western end was destroyed.

The south side wall joined the chimney wall at an obtuse angle.

Its construction was similar to that of the chimney. Six and one-half feet remain, which seems to have been the original length. Near its western extremity the wall became slightly thicker, probably for reinforcement. On the outside corner where wall and chimney met was a vertical recess 4 inches deep in which were the remains of a wooden upright.

The hearth floor was paved with large rectangular flags carefully laid in mortar. The flags varied in size from ½ to 1½ feet, and had a thickness of about 2 inches. The general effect is still extremely pleasing and must have been even more so in its original state. Fire, dampness, and frost had wrought the same effects here as on the chimney wall so that the hearthstones were cracked into numerous small fragments. Moreover, the entire fireplace had settled unevenly with the result that the floor was higher in some places than in others. The hearth was remarkably wide—at the south side, 5 feet and it was 9½ feet long.

One of the first features discovered in excavating west of the fireplace was a stone fall in which the rectangular limestone blocks lay on their narrow sides, with mortar filling the vertical cracks between them. There could be no doubt that this was the upper part of the chimney wall which had collapsed westward, remaining intact in the process so that the stones retained their relative positions. In the higher parts, even the double coursing (of inside and outside blocks) was clearly apparent, so that the construction was identical with the part which remained standing. The fallen stones reached the K^1-line, a distance of 25 feet from the base of the existing wall. This fragment is itself 3 feet high. The total height above ground of the original wall must, therefore, have been at least 28 feet, and probably slightly more (Pl. xx a).

An attempt was made to recover the stones and pile them in proper relative order, but owing to their fragmentary condition this was impossible, and they had to be piled without regard to position.

CYST

In front of the great fireplace, a small rectangular area of black soil showed loose limestone blocks and chips protruding from it. On investigation, this was found to have been an excavation containing on its floor a wooden box or tray-like affair in two sections. On top lay an iron hook. The hole was just large enough to receive the tray or box. Bits of hard-compacted clay suggested that it had been covered with this material originally. There is no indication as to its use, but it is possible that it was a sort of cooling cellar for perishables, and that the tray was for raising and lowering them into the pit. When the place was burned, the chimney of the fireplace collapsed and some of the stone fell into the hole and filled it (Pl. vii *a, b*).

SPECIMENS

A large number of specimens was recovered from the area of the Residence. Some of these were doubtless articles which had fallen through the cracks in the floor during the period of occupation, like the small pins (Pl. xli, G, H) found south of the double fireplace, and the iron fishhook from 77N^1; while the glass beads found near the west sill opposite the great fireplace were more likely lost in the confusion of departure. So also were several iron axes, one with part of the charred wooden handle still in position, and indeed most of the specimens from the area (Pl. v *b*). Noteworthy in this class is a fragment of textile found partly on the sill and partly on charred wood adjacent to it on the west (Pl. xxvii, C). The presence of considerable amounts of bone such as could be left from the table is more difficult to understand. It occurred in small amounts over all the area, but was especially plentiful in the northwest corner, and north of the great fireplace. In most cases the bone was broken into small fragments; some of it had been burned, and of this material a quantity was found in the large hearth. The most abundant class of remains was the hardware—nails, staples, clamps, hinges, hooks, and such unidentifiable objects as concave iron disks (Pl. xxxvii), an iron hook-like object (Pl. xxvi *b*), and perforated sheets of iron. Copper was present in small quantities, but less abundantly than in the workshop area. The most notable copper object was a fragmentary plate found south of the great fireplace. A small amount of European pottery and glass was found also. A few objects of Indian origin came to light, the most conspicuous being a fragmentary ladle of antler which lay along the south wall of the great fireplace, and the textile fragment mentioned above. Charred corn and beans found in greater abundance west and north of the large fireplace and at least some of the discarded bone may be attributed to the Indians.

The specimen list shows, therefore, a wide assortment of materials and finished objects. A certain amount is scrap; some is waste, like the bones; and a large proportion is hardware, of the sort common to all locations of wooden structures on the site. The residue includes household equipment (textiles, pottery, glass, and other articles, indicating such domestic activities as cooking.) There is a marked absence of such workshop débris as iron and copper nuggets and shavings. Some of the specimens pertain to the religious life (beads, rosary fragment), or at least suggest it (copper plate). A few objects like iron axes were probably kept in the house for convenience. But by and large, the specimens, if a little heterogeneous, seem to have been more domestic in nature than definitely pertaining to any one calling such as that of the priest, the carpenter, or the smith.

When excavation began there was nothing to indicate what lay concealed below the sod. There was, it is true, a large and irregular mound of stone upon which the monument stood, mostly covered by dirt and grass, and supporting two large elms. There was also, some 20 feet or more south of the mound as measured from centre to centre, the deep pit which was used as a refuse dump, with a large tree growing at the bottom. The pit was about 3 feet deep and the top of the stone mound about the same height above the general level. The topsoil was extremely thin on level ground; in fact fragments of "burnt clay" could easily be found in certain spots in considerable quantity. In the southwest corner of the Residence the topsoil was about 4 to 10 inches deep and along the 77-line it was of the same thickness. Over the K^1-line there was generally about 3 inches of topsoil beneath which lay a full level of the "burnt clay." Deep concentrations occurred around the great fireplace, as much as 30 inches of it in the southeast corner. Included in this particular mass were several large fragments of a kind of fire-brick, which is described elsewhere (Pl. xxvii b). Beneath the burnt clay lay the charred beams and floor boards. With the wood, generally, was the hardware, and, as could be expected, European articles were found on the floor level. Beneath the level of the floor a few specimens were occasionally discovered, particularly scraps of bone. A very considerable amount of bone was taken out of the 77-squares beneath the burnt clay, usually not closely associated with other materials. A profile, such as that taken between the pit and the mound, showed about 5 inches of humus mixed with brick and overlying sand, and occasionally included lenses of ash and charcoal.

(b) The Chapel

The second largest wooden structure built on the site in Jesuit times was situated immediately north of the Residence, and was so placed that the outer walls of the two buildings formed a straight line, which may have been continuous. The distance between the two structures could not have been greater than 4 feet and may have been much less. On the north it was contiguous with the bastion at the northwest corner. The only internal structure in this building, the fireplace, constituted a wall between it and the bastion, but at the west end of the fireplace, a door from this building gave access to the interior of the bastion. The position was well indicated—on the west by the sill, on the north by the fireplace, and on the south and east by rows of stake-moulds. The dimensions were almost exactly half those of the Residence. From its location, size, and internal characteristics, this building is considered to be the Chapel, so often referred to in the *Jesuit Relations*, and is so designated in this Report (Map 8, B).

The wooden sill on the west side was plainly visible on excavation. Details of its construction were less clear, however, than those of the Residence, possibly because charring had been incomplete. It began with a heavy timber laid at the west side of the door, at right angles to the bastion wall, and continued south to 78L[1]. Excavation beneath the sill revealed two rows of small post- or stake-moulds, the stakes staggered so that they were not opposite to each other (Pl. III *b*). These stakes had supported the sills off the ground to keep them from too rapid decay. They were placed 14 inches apart in rows and the rows themselves were about 4 inches from centre line to centre line. The average diameter was 4 inches. A cut made to determine the depth of those moulds showed that it varied from 12 to 26 inches but averaged about 20 inches (Pl. viii *a*). The moulds were present all along the west sill as far as it went, and their presence was proved likewise under the sill of the Residence.

The south wall was indicated by another double line of stake-moulds following the 78-line to 78P¹. It made a right-angled turn at that point and proceeded north, straddling the P¹ line to the centre of 86P¹. At this place, the intersection of the line of stake-moulds with the line of the north face of the hearth-floor, it made a westerly turn and seemed to continue 1 foot north of the hearth wall (Map 10).

These stake-moulds, of which 116 were counted, outlined three sides of a rectangular building; 20 feet wide from east to west and 40 feet long from north to south. The presence of the stake-moulds and the positions of those on the west side under the sill is strong evidence for the former existence of similar sills on the south and east. Indeed, there were actually fragments of such a sill on the south side and a piece in 85O¹. There is no doubt that the timber at the east side of the Chapel was not burned but rotted away, and the same fate must have overtaken its counterpart on the east side of the Residence.

A secondary arrangement of stake-moulds became apparent 2 feet north and 3½ feet east of 80L¹. From this point they ran north to the 81-line. But at a point 4 feet north of the 80-line they were met by another row of stake-moulds which ran as far east as 80N¹. A third line with with a N-S arrangement was visible here, beginning 2 feet east and 1 foot north of 80N¹, and ending 2½ feet east and 2½ feet north of 81N¹. Or to describe the arrangement more concisely, it formed a broad H, 3 feet high on one side, 6½ feet high on the other, and 10 feet wide. The moulds were of the same sort as under the sills, arranged in much the same positions, with two staggered rows. The arrangement, however, was less systematic, and less easy to understand.

Irregular rows of large flat stones paralleled the north and south sills on the inside of the structure. They lay very close to the centre lines of the L¹ and O¹ squares on the west and east respectively, beginning with 78L¹ and 78O¹ and ending in 82L¹ and 83O¹. The stones were mostly limestone, undressed, but re-

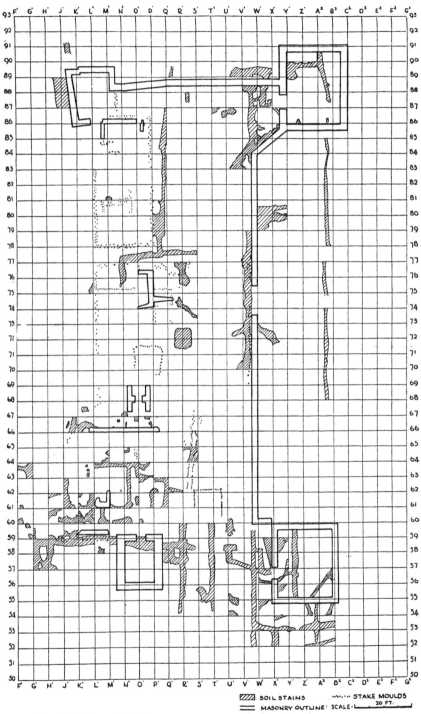

MAP 10. Plan of the European compound, showing the arrangement
of post-moulds and soil markings.

latively flat, and averaged about 14 inches in diameter. They lay
on a thin layer of humus which seemed to have been the original
topsoil and, so far as could be determined, had been placed there
rather than dropped from some higher position. The upper surface
of the stones did not lie in the same plane; some were several
inches higher than others. In square 84L¹, the absolute level of
the top of the sill was 590.33 feet; that of the top of the stones
in 82L¹, 589.88 feet; and the top of the humus level in 83L¹, 589.76

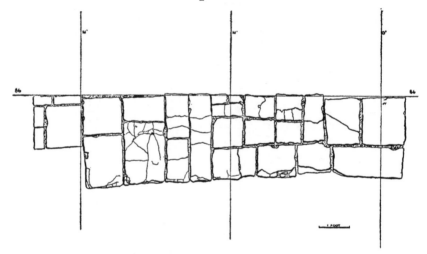

Fig. 7. Plan of Chapel fireplace, showing hearth.

feet. These levels are indicative of the general situation as it was
at the time of excavation, but of course do not necessarily represent it as it was in the seventeenth century. Whatever their purpose, the stones undoubtedly were placed in their present position,
either to carry roof supports or wooden columns (see Pl. viii *b* and
Map 9).

Accessory arrangements of similar stones were apparent near
the south end along the 80- and 81-lines and in the N¹ squares.
They did not, as may be seen from the floor, coincide with the
H-form of stake moulds but seemed to be associated with it in
some way. The stones were generally smaller and more closely
placed. Taken together, the two features—stones and stake-moulds
—suggest some sort of chamber or small compartment within the
Chapel itself.

As already noted, the fireplace for this structure was placed at its north end, where its chimney could form the wall between it and the adjacent bastion. About 3 feet of the lower portion remained standing but there was no orderly stone fall, as in the case of the fireplace previously described, to indicate its height (Map 8, S and Fig. 7). In shape the structure was long and narrow; the chimney wall was 14½ feet long and the side wall at the west end 5 feet. The east side wall was damaged at both ends, and the middle section only about three courses high, so that little could be learned of its original nature. Its existence and position were clear. Walls were constructed similarly to those in the great fireplace of the Residence. The chimney wall showed the same arching, though less conspicuously; and a recess in the northeast exterior corner of the structure for the reception of an upright timber, as already described, had its counterpart in the large fireplace (Pl. x b). The hearth is extraordinarily shallow, in which respect it differs most from the others on the site. At its widest it is but 3 feet, 4 inches; and at the east end even this reduces to 2½ feet. It was composed of beautiful limestone slabs very neatly and carefully laid in about 2 inches of lime mortar. About twenty large and three small slabs were used, and one more was needed to complete the southwest corner. The flags varied from 2 to 3 inches in thickness. The largest were 2¼ feet by 1 foot in size.

A layer of ash containing numerous bone fragments lay on the hearth stones, and above this a patchy layer of charred wood similar to that found on the Chapel area, consisting of the remains of boards and timber. On top of this again was the usual mantle of baked clay, here 13 to 14 inches deep.

This fireplace was designed to heat the building at the northern end of which it was situated. The fact that its flue was in the wall between Chapel and bastion allowed it to provide at least some heat to the latter. The ash and bones indicate that it was used despite its extreme narrowness. A long log could be burned in it safely enough if, as seems to have been the case, there was no wooden floor in the chapel. However, it was probably not used for long, to judge by the relative thinness of the deposit, and by the well-preserved state in which the stones were uncovered. It may be that this fireplace was built late, and was used with the hearth unfinished.

The condition of this area before excavation was very similar to that of the Residence. The topsoil was thin and often nearly all "burnt clay," which was usually present to the third and even fourth levels. In certain places it was heavily concentrated; around the fireplace and in the doorway it attained a depth of 2 feet; it was especially abundant, too, along the lines of stake-moulds and from 82M^1 to 82O^1. Fragments of charred boards were strewn over the area, usually without much semblance of order, since they lay at various angles, and were frequently embedded in the burnt clay. Beneath was a thin layer of humus, as before observed, and under this, sand.

In certain parts, notably just south of the hearth, there appears to have been a partly charred floor, but how extensive it was is impossible to say. Part of the floor could have been charred and the rest might have escaped the fire, only to rot away later. This would account for the light humus line found under the burnt clay over most of the area (Pl. xx b).

The other charred boards which showed no arrangement seem to have come from the roof. Most lay approximately east and west, but many lay at various angles to one another, some crossing over and some under; such remains were more abundant in the western part of the building.

Here, too, the burnt clay appears to have originated as a clay daub applied to walls and roof. Its presence over all the area indicates the latter, and its greater concentration along the walls the former. It may also have been used on the interior of the Chapel as a sort of plaster, otherwise its presence both under and above the boards would be difficult to explain.

Specimens were numerous in the Chapel area but less abundant than in the Residence. Of European material, hardware was again the most abundant, 189 nails, found for the most part near the sills, an iron wedge (Pl. xxiv b), a staple (Pl. xxxiii, G), and two iron angles being the conspicuous items of this class. Important also were an adze (Pl. xlvi, H) and a spear-point with a long slender stem (Pl. xlix, A), both of iron. A copper pin and two glass beads were also found. Indian artifacts included a well-made

stone axe found near the surface of the stone fall above the hearth
(Pl. xxviii *a*), a few potsherds and a chert scraper. Charred plum-
stones and beans, and great quantities of bone may be attributable
to either Indians or Europeans; about 1,000 bone fragments, very
much broken, were picked up from the hearth floor, and other
concentrations of them occurred south of the hearth and at the
south end of the building. They came principally from the lower
levels.

A study of the specimen inventory shows that both native and
European goods were found on the supposed site of the Chapel.
Some of the food remains seemed to antedate its erection, but
some again were certainly coeval with it. Most of the material
was constructional hardware. A large number of iron and copper
specimens, like the adze and the wedge, were utilitarian objects;
some too were probably made for Indian use, such as the long
harpoon-like point. The Indian goods were mostly contemporary
Huron; but the stone axe was undoubtedly later, and possibly
Algonkian. The inventory does not reveal anything which would
conclusively point to the use of the building as a chapel; there
were no crucifixes, altar pieces, or other religious objects. The two
beads do not in themselves prove such use.

It may be asked, then, why this building has been called the
Chapel? There is no passage in the *Relations,* so far as the writer
knows, to support such a theory, and the excavation evidence is
inconclusive. The identification is purely tentative. We do know
that a chapel existed on the site and this building merely seems
to be the one best suited to such use. It was situated at the northwest corner, where it would be least exposed to attack. In size it
was ample to accommodate fifty or sixty people, or the maximum
personnel of the establishment. It appears, moreover, to have
been but a one-storey structure, if the scattered boards came from
the roof as supposed. Position, size, and height point to its being
the most suitable for chapel use.

(c) The Workshop

As previously remarked, the workshop is thought to have
been located between the southwest bastion and the Residence,

since the masonry foundation for a flue was found there, and a great amount of workshop débris, iron and copper scrap and a number of tools.

The flue foundation was situated 10 feet north of the bastion and 25 feet south of the Residence, the south wall of the feature being parallel with the north wall of the bastion, and the west wall parallel and in line with that of the Residence (Map 8, N).

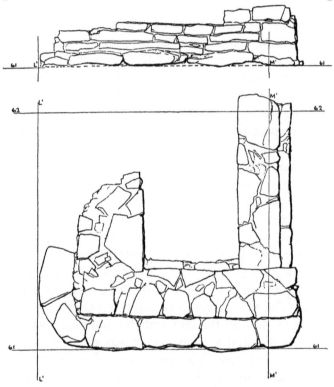

FIG. 8. Plan and elevation of the forge flue.

No superficial marks indicated its presence. On the contrary, the largest elm tree on the entire site was growing on one side of it. This of course had to be laboriously and completely removed, which fortunately caused no additional damage to the structure. It had, however, suffered severely from the passage of time, for nothing more than the foundation courses remained (Pl. xviii, a, b).

The flue foundation consisted of a rectangular base, open on the north side. Carefully cut limestone slabs were laid in mortar with larger slabs forming a rough footing in two courses. The upper structure had three courses intact, measuring from 1 to 1½ feet in thickness and about the same in height. The length of the east, south, and west segments were respectively 6½, 5½, and 3½ feet (Pl. xviii b, Fig. 8).

Around the structure and particularly in square 61M¹ immediately east, an unusually large number of iron tools was found, and some scraps of metal. Square 61M¹ yielded, amongst other things, a blacksmith's hammer (Fig. 14,B), five incomplete axes (Pl. xliv, B, E), and a kind of socket. The level where these were found was almost a solid mass of amorphous charcoal with a good deal of ash. The square southeast of the structure also contained metal goods in quantity; in fact, it afforded one of the most spectacular discoveries of the excavation, for here in level 4 were found eight iron axes in a cluster. Four of these are shown in (Pl. xliii, F, H, and Pl. xliv, D, G). Judging from the position and condition (four of them were relatively undamaged), they had been left hanging on a wall when the settlement was abandoned to the flames—forgotten no doubt in the excitement and despair. They were found exactly as they had fallen. Other metal goods of less interest lay in the same square. The squares north, east, and south of the masonry structure gave evidence of having been part of a building; it is therefore reasonable to conclude that here was the workshop where the smith, Brother Gauber, worked, and that the scraps of metal and tools lying round about were part of the discard material from the bench. The forge itself, if the concentration of charcoal is sufficient evidence, may have occupied square 61M¹ and the flue which it necessitated was doubtless carried on the masonry foundation still extant in 61L¹.

A careful examination of the surrounding area yielded no clues as to the size or position of the building, although there must have been one to house the forge and to serve as a workshop.

(d) The Storage Pit

A slight and irregular depression lay athwart the ditch which ran lengthwise of the ruins, but was inconspicuous enough not to

attract attention. Two small trees grew in it. Upon excavation it
was seen to mark the position of a noteworthy wooden structure
whose construction was probably unique on this continent. It was
situated about 7 feet west of the east curtain, the south ends of
both structures being about in line (Map 8, C).

The first two levels, and in places the first three, consisted
of humus containing a good deal of modern rubbish. Beneath the
humus was 6 inches of sand, then clay. In the fifth level of 62S^1
was found a portion of a log or stick, lying north and south,
which subsequent digging showed was linked up with other
material evidently modern both north and south of it.

Tops of wooden stakes began to appear at a slightly deeper
point in 60S^1 and 62R^1. Careful excavation showed that there
were similar rows of stakes along the east and west sides, but
only one or two individual specimens at the south. When excavation was complete it was apparent that the corner stakes were
larger and better preserved than the others, and that the smaller
ones were wedged into hollow logs which had been set firmly
between the corner posts. The entire structure was approximately
8½ feet square, measured inside. If one adds to this the width of
the horizontal logs, it becomes about 9½ feet. The cell was not
perfectly square, the east side being the longest; nor was it
oriented squarely with the rest of the buildings in the compound,
but instead was placed at a considerable angle to the long axis
of the fortifications (Pl. IX a and b).

The four cedar logs used as sills were much the same size and
shape as the rest. They were apparently left in their original shape,
except that the upper side was flattened and then grooved to
receive the stakes. The heavy corner posts were a foot in diameter,
and stood 1½ feet above the logs. There was no post at the southwest corner. All the posts were badly weathered and had lost
their clear outline, but seemed to have been octagonal in section.
The depth to which they were driven into the ground was not
determined. Forty-eight stakes were still in place, and there had
been at least one more; fifteen on the north side, fourteen on the
west, and eighteen (originally nineteen) on the east. Although
the log in the south was hollowed like the rest to receive stakes,
only one was in existence, and there is no means of knowing if

there had been more. These stakes had been driven into the logs without much care to spacing since some were close together and others wide apart. Diameters ranged from 3 to 6 inches. Five were over 1 or 1½ feet high when uncovered, and most were at least 6 inches high. They seem to have been made from poles with the bark still on, sharpened at one end. When excavated, they were all in a very fragile condition, with most of the fibre disintegrated, leaving only a crumbling mass. The corner posts were much better

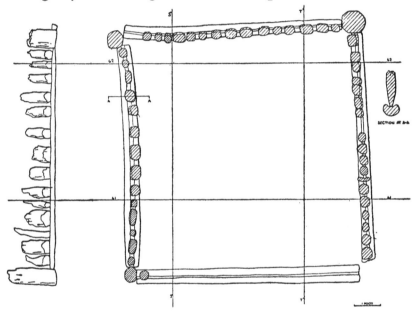

Fig. 9. Plan of the storage pit and elevation of the west side.

preserved (Fig. 9). The stakes were driven into the hollowed logs so as to lean inward slightly, but by no means enough to meet at the top. Some kind of roof must therefore have been necessary, but no vestige of it remains.

Only a space large enough to accommodate it was dug for the structure, as could easily be seen by the cut made into the blue clay. Nor was there any floor. The bottom of the little room was covered all over to a depth of 3 inches with a mass of decayed vegetable matter, full of fibre and seeds. On analysis it showed the presence of seeds of blackberries, wild strawberries, wild grapes, hawthorns, and pin cherries. No European plants were represented. In addition to the above there were great quantities of squash seeds, mostly concentrated in the mass of vegetal matter piled up against the stakes. The presence of such remains suggests that the place was a storage pit. It may, of course, have begun life as a storage pit, and been converted later, perhaps when it fell into disrepair, into a refuse pit. At any rate, a quantity of refuse such as scraps of iron, a red glass bead, a copper pin or needle, two broken glass bottles, the leg bones of a domestic cock, and other bones, found chiefly in the western half of the structure, could bear no relation to storage.

Fortification Structures

(a) The Southwest Bastion

This, the smallest of all four bastions, was a crater-like mound of stones when excavations began (Map 8, D). It was about 3 feet above the ground level and about 25 feet wide. A small tree grew out of the pile near the southeast corner, one inside at the northwest corner, and three large ones on the east slope of the mound. As will be seen from a study of the photographs, the mound itself was a mass of fallen stones drifted over with a generous coating of sand and leaf-mould (Pl. xi a).

Excavation involved removing the dirt and the stone, while watching for the original floor or ground level. The exterior slopes seemed not to be disturbed; but the bottom of the crater was in a confused state, so much so in fact as to lead to the conclusion that some previous digger had worked there as far down as floor level. Only the centre of the floor was disturbed.

Measured inside, the bastion was 14 feet long from north to south and 11 feet wide. The thickness of the walls averaged 1½ feet. In addition to this the footing, of unascertained depth, protruded 4 inches beyond the wall both inside and out. The height of the walls above the footing was about 4 feet. Granite boulders, roughed into shape, and a few limestone blocks were the building material. The outer surfaces were moderately flat. It was estimated that about one-half of the granite boulders showed some cutting and trimming. The stones were mostly laid in courses, although in some places no coursing was evident. The surfaces of the walls, both inside and out, were composed of large stones, though not large enough to overlap (Fig. 10). Hence a "hearting" of small stones and chips was built up. The corners were fashioned of large, flat limestone blocks, as much as 25 inches by 7 inches by 5 inches in size, roughly bonded together (Pl. IV a). Lime mortar was used as the bonding agent; while it is now in a weak condition, it must originally have been of good quality. The lower 2 feet of the walls, particularly the south wall, showed traces of a hard, white plaster on both inside

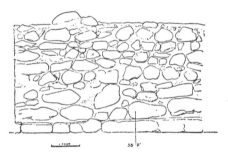

FIG. 10. The inner face of the east wall of the southwest bastion, showing the nature of the masonry.

and outside surfaces. Even the footing along the inside of the south wall showed a 2-inch coating of plaster in some places. Details of masonry construction may be seen in Pl. XI b and XII a.

The only opening was a doorway placed a little east of the centre in the north side. The ends of the walls abutting on the door were not carefully finished; on the contrary they presented the same appearance as would a cross-section made at any other point through them. The threshold was but 4 inches higher than the top of the footing. The width of the door was 3 feet (Pl. XII b). There were remains of a plank threshold, completely charred. Interestingly enough, a cluster of fish bones lay on it, remnants evidently of some hasty repast. Threshold and frames, of which fragments were in position, were 1 foot wide. The elevation of the doorstep was 589 feet.

Fragments of charred boards running east and west appeared here and there above the inside footing. It was assumed that they were part of the floor, partly from their nature and position and partly because six large iron spikes and six nails were found with them at the same level. None of the boards was sufficiently well preserved to permit the taking of measurements. Beneath the floor there was a soil pattern, the principal features of which were dark patches on sand at the north side and southeast corner, converging towards the east. They were probably due to partial clearing or levelling of the ground preparatory to building.

In addition to the nails and spikes already mentioned, a small number of specimens lay inside the bastions, chief of which were a conical copper bangle, a flint core, a few lumps of copper and iron, and a quantity of bone. The amount of stone collected from the ruins of this bastion and adjacent small structures was 1,237 cubic feet. Probably as much as 90 per cent of this came from the bastion. The total amount would be sufficient to rebuild the walls 11 feet above their present height.

This bastion, though one of the best preserved, is the smallest of all four. For some reason, it tilts slightly to the east, and since no cracks have developed, seems to have been so built. Father Martin describes this bastion as a "construction carré qui formait peut-être la base d'une tour du haut de laquelle on pouvait voir au loin et surveiller les approches."[*] Since he makes no mention of having investigated his "tower," it is likely that the disturbance of the floor, already mentioned, dates from a later time. At any rate, it is now fairly certain that the structure was indeed a bastion, despite the fact that it was 8 feet east of the corner of the compound.

(b) The Southeast Bastion

The southeast bastion also appeared before excavation as a large mound of stone and dirt with a deep crater (Map 8, E). At its highest point it stood about 3½ feet above the level of its surroundings, a little less than the bastion just described, but it covered a larger area, and four trees grew on its periphery. The crater contained, besides fallen stones and dirt, a large amount

[*]Martin, *Voyages et recherches*, p. 66.

of débris such as broken china, plastics, rubber, and all the other rubbish which marks a modern dump heap.

As before, the stones were piled separately from this structure, and a watch kept for unusual features and for specimens. The centre of the crater had been disturbed just as in the southwest bastion, but because of the greater area here, there was relatively less destruction. A stratigraphic column was left in the southeast corner.

This was a large bastion, 21 feet north and south, by 17 feet east and west, measured inside. The walls averaged 2 feet in thickness and the footing extended 4 to 5 inches beyond this again both inside and out, making it slightly more massive than its southwestern counterpart. The nature of construction was the

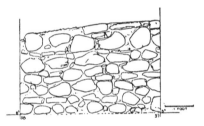

Fig. 11. The inner face of the east wall of the southeast bastion, show-ing the nature of the masonry.

same, however, except that here more granite boulders were used (about 80 per cent of the total) and less limestone; indeed the latter was used only in small courses for chinking. The interior footing on the south side was particularly well made, consisting of very even-sized granite boulders (Fig. 11). The walls were in a moderately good state of repair, standing for the most part to a height of 4 feet, and in some to 5, except that a large break occurred at the southwest corner. It extended for 5 feet along the south wall and took in about 2 feet of the west wall. The stones from it were buried deep in the surrounding soil, suggesting that it was a very early break. Even part of the footing was destroyed, which makes it difficult to think that the damage was done in recent times.

Seven feet north of the southwest corner there began a door-way which was 3½ feet wide. It had suffered a good deal, and the stones had slumped inward. The threshold was 23 inches above the footing; it was peculiar in having a lengthwise row of 8-inch to 10-inch stones, perhaps the only remains of a flat doorstep. There were but faint indications of a wooden frame.

The interior, near the walls, was undisturbed and on excavation revealed ample evidence of wooden flooring, supported a little above the level of the footing. An almost continuous piece existed in the northeast corner, along with larger pieces which were probably timbers. It was all so completely reduced to charcoal that very little could be ascertained about its structure.

An unusual feature of this bastion was a stone buttment or platform extending southward from the north wall in squares 58Y^1 and 59Y^1. It was slightly over 2 feet wide and 5 feet long, rectangular in form, and stood 9 inches above the top of the footing. It was built of limestone blocks worked to shape. Its edges were irregular. Beneath the large top stones lay small slabs of limestone which protruded around the sides. The purpose of this structure is unknown (Pl. xiii a), but it may have served as a footing for a staircase.

Between the platform and the west wall was a small cedar log beneath which was a charred board and fragment of "burnt clay." Limestone chips lay round about and northward was a small bed of lime. It was apparent here that stones had fallen directly upon the planks. Numerous nails, an iron spike, and a hinge were obtained, chiefly from the last-mentioned feature, and the flooring in the northeast corner, but there were very few other specimens. Eighteen hundred cubic feet of stone, or enough to add 12 feet to the existing walls, was recovered from the interior and immediate vicinity.

This, the second largest of the bastions, resembled two others in being rectangular and in having its north-south axis the longer. Like these, moreover, it possessed a substantial footing; and a doorway opening upon the interior of the compound. Situated at the south end of the curtain and 5 feet east of it, it was in a position to sweep the east side of the establishment with gun-fire in case of need. The peculiar stone buttment built inside the north wall and the serious breach at one corner differentiated this bastion from the others.

(c) The Northeast Bastion

The original mound concealing the northeast bastion exceeded all others in size, with average diameters of 35 and 40 feet and a height of nearly 5 feet above the general level. It had, however, the common crater-like form. Drifting soil which had accumulated on the fallen rubble and stones supported a meagre growth of grass and weeds. In externals it did not differ materially from other structures of its kind. It supported four trees (Map 8, F).

The amount of fallen stone around this bastion was the same as around the bastion just described, that is 1,800 cubic feet, enough to add 7 feet to the existing walls. It would appear that the upper parts of the walls must have fallen soon after the fire, because many large stones fell upon and broke through the floor. Also, the north wall when uncovered leaned outward precariously with a resultant break at the northeast corner. Other walls were reasonably well preserved.

On inside measurement, the unit was 18½ feet from east to west and 23 feet from north to south, the largest of its type in the complex. The walls were 2½ feet thick, supported on a footing 10 inches wider than themselves. Great care had been taken in building them. Into a trench of appropriate size heavy timbers, thought to be cedar, were placed lengthwise; upon them the footing was constructed, 27 inches deep and 40 inches wide, with very large granite boulders at the bottom and smaller ones in higher courses. The timber was 4 inches thick by 12 inches wide, and two were laid side by side to provide a sufficient base for the footing. In its upper portions the footing showed some evidence of having been plastered. The wall itself consists in its lower courses of large granite boulders a foot thick and of various lengths; but in its upper courses of smaller stones, all laid in lime mortar. The highest point of standing wall was 57 inches, and the average height 4 feet all around, except for the damaged corner already mentioned.

An unusually large opening (74 inches wide) occurred in the west wall immediately south of the curtain, providing passage back and forth between the interior of the compound and the bastion. The threshold was 18 inches above the top of the footing, so that there must either have been a floor near it or steps up to it from near ground level. The doorway, if such it should be called, had certain peculiarities. Charred wood, presumably from the frame, lay in the masonry. At the south end, however, was a 25-inch space which was free of charcoal, but appeared instead to have been plastered. At this point the threshold was the full width of the wall, that is, 27 inches; southward, the masonry contracted to a width of 20 inches, the remaining space being taken up with timbers laid into the recess thus created in the wall, as indicated by the charcoal with the grain running east and west still in place.

That the bastion had been provided with a floor was suggested by the quantity of charcoal distributed over the area. No boards were in position or measurable, so that the existence of a floor cannot be definitely asserted. Fallen timbers were common around the sides, particularly on the northwest corner.

A considerable number of specimens was found at or near floor level. Besides the usual nails, there were three iron axes and an axe socket, three large spikes, a copper instrument somewhat like a diminutive set square (Pl. L, D) about ninety fragments of bone, several plum-stones, a few beans, a kernel of maize, and a quantity of pottery-like material. The latter and some of the nails came from a "bonfire"-like formation near the centre of the east wall. The "pottery" is seemingly amorphous, although it has the consistency of earthenware and a greenish glaze. Two of the axes lay near the "bonfire," the third was in the southeast corner.

The two eastern bastions formed a pair for the protection of the eastern exposure of the settlement. Like its counterpart, this one was set out from the east curtain, to which it was linked by an angled wall, and it projected some 10 feet north of the north curtain. It seems unlikely, however, that it was intended to provide protection on the north, other than incidentally; its main function must have been to guard the east. The west wall of the bastion and the north curtain met at a 90° angle, but they remained separate entities. The wall which linked the bastion with the east curtain forms an angle of 135° with each, and it was likewise left unbonded.

(d) The Northwest Bastion

This unit when first seen presented an appearance of extreme disintegration. The fallen stones which marked its position made but a small mound, if such it could be called. At the south side the pile was 3 feet high; at the centre it was somewhat depressed but lacked the definitely crater-like formation of other bastions. It was, in short, relatively inconspicuous and densely overgrown.

There appeared to be an element of danger in removing any material whatsoever from the area without definite proof that it was extraneous. By following the north curtain, this difficulty was overcome to some extent, and it was possible to trace out the outlines of the structure. As will be explained below, the walls and the curtain wall were not built solidly or carefully as in other bastions. Hence the nature of construction was not in itself sufficient to identify the unit; position and shape were the only criteria.

The northwest bastion was irregular in shape and poor in construction. It was, in fact, but an enlargement of a corner rather than a separate entity; for the curtain wall merely turned north for 6 feet, then west for 9 feet, and with a slight jog continued west for another 3½ feet. At this point it ran south for 14 feet, then turned eastward. The south wall was in line with the chimney wall of the Chapel fireplace. Approximate inside dimensions were 15 feet from north to south, by 12½ feet from east to west, as measured from the west wall to the end of the north curtain; if, however, one includes the area north of the fireplace in the bastion, as one probably should, then the greatest east-west length was 23 feet. The great irregularity and almost tentative nature of construction may easily be seen. Details of shape and dimensions are apparent on the diagram (Map 8, G).

The 5- foot section of the east wall varied in thickness from 16 to 21 inches. The other walls were equally variable. The west wall was 26 inches. In general, these walls were composed of large stones on the outside with small ones on the inner face, notably in the west segment; in other places only small stones were used. The west wall had a footing of medium-sized stones, but no other wall showed a similar structure. There was no evidence of retaining stakes such as were seen along the east curtain.

Only a small volume of stone was collected from the bastion area, but still enough to add 6 feet to the height of the walls, or a total of 432 cubic feet. It is doubtful if the nature of construction employed in this particular unit would allow the walls to be carried higher than that, unless interior supports such as were used for curtain walls were resorted to. At all events, it is apparent that the original amount of stone was smaller than for any of the other bastions, and that the walls were thinner and likely of lesser height. It is nevertheless possible that a certain amount may have been removed in recent times by people who felt themselves in need of building stone.

The doorway between the south wall segment and the fireplace has already been referred to. Originally it was filled with brick-like material lying beneath large stones. When cleared, it was found to be 33 inches wide and as deep as the walls were thick, that is 27 inches. The northwest corner of the chimney wall was recessed, the depth of the recess being 14 inches from north to south, and the width 4½ inches; an 8-inch fragment of post or frame was in position. No frame remained on the west side. A board, or more properly two boards, 2 feet long and 14 inches wide constituted the threshold.

A thin layer of humus and charcoal dust suggested that the interior had been floored, although no actual boards remained. Scattered timbers lying here and there on the interior area very likely fell from the roof. The case was different with the space between the north curtain and the fireplace, for it was almost entirely covered with charred boards and timbers. The boards ran E-W and varied in width from 5 inches to 1 foot. Crossing these, and apparently on top of them, were three timbers, hollow on their upper sides and 7 or 8 inches wide. Since the boards were on the under side of the timbers, they must all have fallen from a ceiling; the remarkable thing is that they fell in such regular formation. This construction could possibly have been traced eastward to the line of the eastern sill of the Chapel had it not been for a tree root which destroyed the evidence at that point (Pl. xiv a).

Besides large numbers of bone fragments and some iron scrap, many interesting specimens were found in the bastion and the area north of the Chapel fireplace. A remnant of iron sieve lay in the southwest corner of the bastion in a mass of ash and charcoal. Near the west wall was a well-made iron knife-blade, an iron tool of unknown use, and a screw nail. There were many nails in the bastion area. But by far the most interesting find was a sewing kit discovered just beneath the charred boards north of the fireplace. It contained a pair of scissors, a pair of tweezers, two fragments of tweezers, a stiletto, and an embossed silver needle case containing the remains of several iron needles (Fig. 20).

There is nothing about this northwest bastion to indicate great protective value. Its walls were weak, apparently built in haste, and even altered in the course of construction. It would seem to have been the original intention of the builders to make them as strong as any others, for they took care to provide a substantial footing for the west wall; but after construction began, the need for haste seems to have forced them to lower the quality of workmanship and to forego serious planning. (Pl. xiii b). Nor was the bastion set out from the corner of the fortifications and made a complete unit in itself. On the contrary, it was merely an enlarged corner, possibly fitted out for living quarters, with only a semblance of strength. The thickness of the walls and the amount of stone remaining on the spot point to its having been only one storey high. The nature of the specimens found in it indicates its use for domestic purposes. The adjacent area to the east was most likely integral with it, and finished as a room.

Martin noticed in connection with this bastion that a wall on the south side ran deep into the interior of the fort; in reality what he saw was the base of the chimney. He further records that digging revealed, at a depth of about 2 feet, a foundation and traces of a burnt floor, large floor nails, a beaver bone, and a piece of copper which he believed had come from some kitchen utensil.

(e) The North Curtain

The north curtain is that element which linked the two northern bastions and provided protection in the northern quarter. It could not be clearly discerned before excavation, covered as it was by soil, scattered stones, vines, and weeds. The remains were principally of stone, with some evidence of accessory features of wood (Map 8, H; Pl. xxⅢ *a*).

Upon exposure the curtain was seen to be intact for an average height of 2 feet. The width was 2½ feet and the length 56 feet. As already remarked, the western end merged with the bastion wall; in the east it ended flush with the wall of the northeast bastion but was not bonded to it in any way. Large undressed boulders of granite were employed, those on the outer side being only slightly larger than those on the inside. They were held together with lime mortar, but showed no trace of arrangement in courses, or of surface finishing (Pl. xⅣ *b*).

Although no supporting stakes could be seen there were three large notches on the inner face of the wall containing the charred remains of stout beams. They occurred in squares 88Q[1], 88V[1], and 88W[1] at a uniform height of about 1 foot above the base of the wall. The first-mentioned was largest, 12 inches wide and 8 inches deep. Charred wood filled the space completely and extended 11 inches south from the wall. The niche in 88U[1] contained a beam of almost the same size. In every case, mortar and small stones had been used to chink in the spaces around the timber.

A number of charred pieces of wood resembling boards and small logs lay in N-S positions near the wall and west of the well, with a few even farther west. Specimens were concentrated near the wall. There were comparatively few south of the 87-line. Iron nails were abundant, but the more interesting specimens included the blade of a hoe or mattock (Pl. xxv *b*), and an iron hook not unlike a doorlatch.

There was no evidence of a door or gate throughout the length of the north curtain. However, it appears that the central ditch had been taken into account in building the wall. Where it interrupted the curtain, its sides were reinforced with planks and the masonry carried across on top, so that the ditch remained functional. The masonry above the ditch eventually settled, presumably after its wooden supports decayed. The amount of subsidence was, however, not very great and resulted in no serious cleavage in the wall.

Enough stone was recovered to add 2½ feet to the present

height of the wall; this is, to build it to a total height of about 5½ feet.

(f) The East Curtain

The east curtain was the protective element on the east side of the compound. In its final condition before excavation, it could be seen as a raised line against which soil had drifted and lodged, more especially against its western face. Some of the stones of which it was composed could still be seen protruding above the soil while others lay round about, making its detection a relatively easy matter (Map 8, J).

As will already have been gathered, the curtain was a straight line lying almost north and south, with two eastward extensions which brought it into contact with the bastion walls. The straight section measured 120½ feet; the north arm, 23½ feet, and the south arm 8 feet, a total of 152 feet, as measured on the west face. The north arm made an angle of 60 degrees with the wall; the south arm an angle of 90 degrees. The former, as already described, joined flush with the south wall of the northeast bastion at its western end but was not bonded to it. The south side of the south arm was in line with the north side of the north wall of the bastion in that quarter, so that the corners met but were not joined (Pl. xv a). This circumstance bespeaks either haste in construction or an error in planning. The only break in the curtain occurred slightly north of centre where the 10-foot wide portal was situated.

The builders cleared away all but about one-half inch of top-soil before beginning construction. They then laid large field boulders, mostly of granite, on the outer side so that their exterior faces made an approximately straight line. The inner face was built up with smaller stones laid in mortar but not coursed or otherwise arranged. The width of the wall, nearly uniform throughout, was 32 inches, although a slight batter on the exterior gave the base somewhat more than this. It remained standing to the height of 2 feet, and enough stone lay round about to bring it up to 3 feet.

The best preserved section was the arm connecting with the northeast bastion; its minimum height was 2 feet above ground level and its maximum 3½ feet. The stones in the outside were the largest of the entire wall; the cobblestones in the interior side were still well preserved in position. Wooden stakes driven into the ground to support the inner face were partially preserved. The extremely haphazard way in which the wall abuts on the bastion masonry indicates that it was built after the latter.

Retaining stakes were found also in various places along the interior face, making it clear that they had once been virtually continuous there. They were usually 4 inches wide, and spaced 4 inches apart from centre to centre. The exceedingly fragmentary remains are probably cedar wood. None exceeded 5 inches in length (Pl. xv b). Additional wooden construction was present in the form of board flooring, not found continuously throughout the length of the curtain, but reasonably uniformly along the interior of the south half, where conditions for its preservation seem to have been better than farther north. Individual boards measured from 9 to 21 inches in width; they lay close to the inside of the wall and parallel to it. Portions of small timbers lay in an E-W or SE-NW direction. It seems obvious that some sort of floor existed here, perhaps a sentry walk originally elevated above ground level; the maximum width of the remains is about 2 feet, but the walk was likely wider than this originally. The presence of a flooring and of retaining stakes, and the modest height to which the fallen stone would permit the curtain to be rebuilt, as well as other factors, point to the existence of a wooden super-structure above the stone foundations.

The portal or gate constituted a 10-foot wide interruption to the curtain wall in squares 73V^1, 74V^1, and 75V^1 (Map 8, K). A charred post, tolerably well preserved, protruded from the soil 8 inches south of the 74 line. South of it again was a fragmentary board, 13 inches wide, 7 inches high, and 2 inches thick, placed on its side and at right angles to the line of the wall; its purpose was either to retain the corner of the wall, or to serve as a door jamb. Similar features were met with at the north side of the opening, where there was a board 6 inches wide and the same height as before. Nearby lay two large spikes and 15 nails.

There were rather more loose stones at the sides of the openings than along the rest of the curtain, and they seemed to lie in a fan-shape on the inner side. A clay fill ran the entire length of the curtain, adjacent to its inner face. It was 10 inches wide, bordered on its western edge by an irregular brown line an inch wide. It was not interrupted by the portal; in this section, the eastern edge was bordered with a similar dark band, obviously due to decayed wood. In some places, remains of what looked like upright planks could be detected along the edges. At both sides of the gate, on the west, is a crescentic clay fill swinging back upon the curtain; in structure and composition it is not unlike the fill parallel to the wall.

(g) The False Wall

A feature rather more interesting for the light it throws upon seventeenth-century local conditions than for its own sake was a row of stones between the two eastern bastions in the A^2 squares (Map 8, Y). Nowhere was the line more than 1½ feet wide, or more than one stone high. It was not continuous in the sense that one stone touched another, but there was no mistaking its linear nature. Small field boulders were laid in an irregular line upon the ground which had been cleared of topsoil (Pl. XVI a).

Evidently this line was intended to be the curtain which was finally built about 20 feet farther west. How far its building progressed is not apparent; but it is either rudimentary or vestigial and most likely the former. We may ask if the final position was due to an actual change in plan, or to a mistake on someone's part, but we can only guess that the latter is the more probable explanation.

(h) Wall Fragment 1

As shown in Fig. 12, a short section of stone wall projected west from the northwest corner of the southwest bastion, in a manner not unlike that in which the south arm of the east curtain touched the bastion in that quarter. In both cases, the southern corners of the walls merely touch the northern corners of the bastions. The one here described was so overlain with large stones like those of which it was composed that it nearly passed unnoticed, since only the bottom course remained (Map 8, L).

The measured length was 10 feet, and the width 2½ feet. In

manner of construction this wall fragment resembled the east curtain, that is, large stones constituted the outer and small ones the inner face; they were also field stones laid in mortar. Two small pieces of timber or board about 2 feet apart and about 6 inches wide and 10 inches long, protruded from under the stones on the north side. Three, or possibly five, stakes or posts made a row along the wall, about a foot south of it; they varied in diameter from 4 to 10 inches (Pl. xvi *b*).

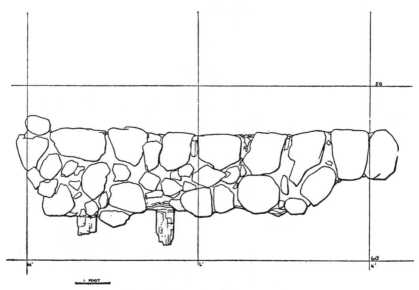

FIG. 12. Plan of wall fragment 1.

This segment was apparently the vestige of an outer wall similar to the east curtain, which it so closely resembled in construction, placement, and union with its bastion. It ended approximately 5 feet west of the line of the Residence sill.

(*j*) Wall Fragment 2

Large and irregularly cut limestone blocks built haphazardly into a sort of wall were encountered in the second level in squares 64K^1 to 65K^1. The construction, which was roughly mortared, measured 10 feet in length and 20 inches in width, and was in line with the western limits of the Residence (Pl. xvii *a*). The soil surrounding it was in a confused condition, just as was the area between the Residence and the southwest bastion. A large deposit of ash lay west of the wall, and quantities of scrap iron and copper near by. Other material included chert, bone, and burnt clay, while at the north end, at a depth of 1 foot was the remains of a hen's egg (Map 8, M).

ACCESSORY FEATURES

The moat system very likely served the triple purposes of water road, defence, and drainage, so that to classify it arbitrarily under one or other of these headings seems undesirable. It has consequently been included with the well and the central ditch under the somewhat inadequate caption of "Accessory Features." These, together with the constructions already described, constituted the physical arrangements of the European compound in so far as remains of them survived.

(a) The Well

Before excavation, a deep hollow was a conspicuous feature of the north part of the enclosure. When first seen it was overgrown with grass and weeds, and contained many large boulders and some wooden sticks. The bottom of the pit was fully 2 feet below the general level of the area. Local tradition had it that this was a well, and such it turned out to be. As already noted, Galbraith's is the only early plan which showed it, and he was of the opinion that it was new. It is said that the bore was but recently filled in, and that because a team of horses had fallen into it.

The Jesuit Fathers must have experienced a need for a well inside the compound, and it is reasonable to believe they constructed one. Since no other possibility was found, this is in all likelihood the one which they made. If this is true, the well at Ste Marie must be the first such structure in what is now Ontario.

Its placement is just inside the north curtain, half-way between the two bastions (Map 8, T). Examination showed that it had two main divisions: an upper rectangular excavation, and a round bore below it. The outlines of the rectangular part were vague because of weathering. Its diameter was not more than a foot and a half greater than that of the bore. A wooden platform presumably covered it, as in modern wells; or it may have been provided with a well-sweep.

The centre of the bore was 11 feet south of the curtain; its eastern edge virtually coincided with the western edge of the ditch. The diameter was 5 feet. The walls of the bore were almost perfectly preserved; in fact the original spade-marks could be dimly distinguished. As the fill of humus, clay, and débris was removed, water began to seep in. By the time the twenty-third level was reached, the flow was so great as to render it impossible to keep a dry footing, and when left over-night, the well partly filled with water. Since there was no means of keeping it dry, it was not excavated beyond a depth of 9 feet. The spring is not now strong enough to fill the well to the top, and if it was no stronger in the seventeenth century, a pump or sweep would have been needed to bring the water to the top.

There was no curbing. It is said that old wells of the nineteenth century still in use in the region were not provided with curbing and are giving satisfaction; so there is no reason why this early well may not have been of the same construction.

Surprisingly few specimens came to light, partly no doubt because the bottom was not reached. The fourth level yielded a brass key and a piece of wire, probably modern, and the twenty-first level a large piece of charcoal and three lumps of badly corroded iron. Three stakes which protruded from the fill seemed to be intrusive.

In conclusion, it appears that this well dates probably from Jesuit times, although there is no positive proof. It was somewhat more than 9 feet deep, with a 5-foot circular bore, without curbing of any kind, in the manner of modern wells.

(b) Central Ditch

Reference has already been made in several places to a depression or ditch running lengthwise of the compound some 15 feet west of the east curtain. It could be clearly seen before excavation; indeed, it is visible in some of the photographs taken during the survey of the site (Pl. 1 b). It became clearly defined at least 10 feet north of the north curtain, beneath which it could easily be traced, and continued south through the S^1 squares to the main moat. It was not so apparent, however, between the latter feature and the 53-line; while beyond the 58- and the 62-lines there were large depressions which spread over the intervening squares to east and west. North of the 63-line it was less interrupted, but nowhere was it more than moderately straight. For instance, its western edge meandered from side to side through the R^1 squares from the 69- to the 83-lines. Moreover, the well outline interfered with the contours of the ditch near it. Accumulation of débris marred and obscured the southern extremity. But for all its dilapidation and irregularity it was still plainly visible (Map 8, V).

Inside the north curtain, the west side of the ditch was clearly marked by a wooden board running north and south and lying on its narrow edge, which continued under the wall. Two and one-half feet east of this was a dark-brown line of rotten wood where a similar board had been. Between the two was a dark patch of humus and sand overlying a thin stratum of water-laid sand. The wall was obviously built across the ditch while it was still open and presumably in use, because it had slumped and settled at that point with consequent damage to itself when the wood beneath rotted and gave way. In the humus in this part of the ditch were found iron nails, copper scraps, charcoal, bone, and, most notable of all, a concave iron disk. Southward the course of the ditch coincided closely with the surface contours. The deepest part of the channel, however, kept close to the east curtain all the way down.

There are indications that Indians made use of the protection afforded by the deeper part of the ditch for building their camp fires. This was especially true in squares $67R^1$ to $67S^1$ where there were several charred boards probably used for additional shelter or for ground covering, and numerous potsherds and fragments of clay pipes. Enough sherds of one pot were found to piece together a large fragment. The ware was typically Huron, as were the pipes. It seems highly unlikely that Indians would be permitted to camp on the ditch while the establishment was occupied, so that either a few Hurons found shelter here in the last few weeks of the existence of the place, or wandering Iroquois, using stolen goods, occupied the spot for a short time after the exodus.

The ditch grew wider between the 62- and 71-lines, expanding towards the west. Excavation showed that there were two channels on the 64-line, one in 64R[1] and the other in 64S[1], and the same condition existed in the squares south. Furthermore, this stretch revealed the presence of two rows of wooden stakes approximately 15 inches apart. They appeared on the 63-line, where they were virtually centred in square 63R[1], and ended just east of stake 68S[1] on the 68-line. At least fifty stakes or stake-moulds could be counted, and if excavation had been carried down as far in other squares as in 65R[1], more might have come to light. Appearing first in levels 6 to 11, they continued to level 18 for a depth of 6 feet. Originally the stakes must have come close to or even above the surface. One well-preserved fragment made of cedar had the lower end sharpened to a point.

The rows lost definition beyond the limits already mentioned. Very likely they continued in both directions originally, forming some sort of retaining wall along the sides of the west channel in the ditch. Indeed, remains of a strip of wood or plank were actually present above the eastern line of stakes at its south end in square 63R[1], level 7. The purpose of the retaining wall here is not clear.

South of the feature just described the ditch opened out into a large basin, closing again to about normal size in squares 60R[1] to S[1] to T[1]. Investigation showed that at the bottom of the large basin was a wooden structure, which for lack of a better name has been called a storage pit (see pp. 61-4). It lay squarely athwart the continuous or eastern channel of the ditch. Moreover, the channel did not cross above the storage pit; instead, it is definitely interrupted by that feature, which must therefore be later in date of construction.

Immediately south of the storage pit were two boards lying on their sides, almost parallel to each other and 2½ feet apart. Although they happen to coincide in position with the ditch, they seem to belong with the storage pit. The best explanation seems to be that they were retaining boards along the sides of a narrow passage-way into that structure (Pl. xxi b).

South of the passage-way the water-laid sand becomes apparent again, but the section between passage-way and moat appears to have been much disturbed subsequent to the time when the ditch was in actual use, for fills cross it in various directions. It seems to have debouched into the main moat along the west side of 54S[1].

That this feature just described was once a water course is fairly certain from the occurrence of water-laid sand on the bottom of its channel. Moreover, while it was not by any means uniform in width, it did possess a definite gradient from north to south, estimated at 3½ feet, between the two ends of the compound. The terrain north of the site has been so greatly altered in recent times that it is impossible to say what the drainage system originally was in that quarter. It is possible, however, that there was enough seepage in ancient times to make a drainage ditch across the level side of the fort very desirable, and there seems no reasonable doubt that the feature under discussion served as such. That it was constructed at an early date is obvious since it antedates the north curtain, the "root cellar," and probably the well. The ditch also antedates the moats, for when these were built they completely drained the terrain. The drying up of the water course thus enabled the French to build the storage pit in its former path.

(c) Moat System

The system of moats has already been mentioned; and it has been remarked that certain parts are extant, others obliterated. Of the former, there were two segments—namely, the main moat, which ran at right angles to and joined the river, and a smaller trench parallel with and near to the west side of the European compound, which joined the main moat at its northern extremity. Those segments which, according to some evidence, surrounded the Indian compound no longer exist. The central ditch appears to be older than the moats, and to have been superseded functionally by them; it is not, for these reasons, included in the system. A study of Maps 3, 4, 5, 8, and 11 will help to make much of the detail clearer.

I. THE MAIN MOAT

Beginning at the river's edge (Pl. xxi a), the main moat ran east for 20 feet, swung slightly north, continued in its easterly course, then ran along the south side of the Residence compound, and ended between the two south bastions (Map 8, W). The eastern portion was conspicuous for two enlargements or basins, one of them south of the southwest bastion and the other immediately west of it. The moat terminated in a shallow enlargement thought to be a third basin.

This defensive work suffered considerable damage, particularly in recent years; its sides have been eroded and the bottom filled in. Rubbish was dumped in the eastern end and elsewhere. To bring spring water to the lodge a trench was dug for a pipe-line within the channel of the moat for part of its length. The reservoir into which the pipe empties drains westward through the rest of the moat. The construction of the driveway involved the filling in of a section. Finally, the portion south of the field was evidently partially filled in, either by deepening the channel and throwing up the dirt on the north side, or by dragging soil off the field. The cut made along the U-line revealed an extensive fill consisting of such modern refuse as cow bones, glass, old garments, wood and metal, the whole covered over with humus and crudely faced with limestone blocks to check erosion. Only when these various mutilations are allowed for can a reasonably clear reconstruction of the main moat be made.

The enlargement or basin in which the moat terminated at its eastern extremity was shallow and ill-defined. Its dimensions were estimated, however, at a length of 30 feet and a width of 14 feet. The central basin had approximately the same size and shape, while the westernmost was the largest of the three with a length of 27 feet and a width of 25 feet from east to west.

Cuts made across the moat and across the basins threw much light on their construction. Three were made: one along the P^1 line, one through the central basin, and the other along the H^1 line. Each provided evidence of the width and depth along these sections, and threw some light on their history.

The first-mentioned cut gave a cross section of the easternmost construction, just before it expands into the terminal basin. About

15 inches of modern humus overlay a stratum of sand, which in turn rested on the original excavation. A sand-filled post-mould was present at each side, showing clearly that stakes had been driven all along the sides of the moat in its upper portions, to serve as a retaining wall. The width of the channel between these points was 9 feet.

The second trench was made rather nearer the western than the eastern end of the centre basin, on the L¹ line. The stratification was similar to that above described; it is well shown in Figure 13. Retaining stakes were also present here, the distance between them being 9 inches. Unlike the first cut, however, this one revealed a secondary channel situated at the centre of the basin and parallel with the moat itself; the secondary channel was 15 inches below the bottom of the basin and had a width of 18 inches.

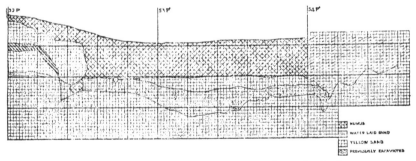

FIG. 13. Profile through the main moat, along the L¹-line.

The third cut made along the H¹ line was chosen to indicate the nature of a side, as well as the central, portion of the largest basin. It showed essentially the same features as in the last with the addition of a row of stake-moulds along the eastern wall. This feature leads to the conclusion that the walls of the basins as well as those of the moat were retained with a stockade of stakes.

The gradient of the original channel south of the compound was 3.9 : 100 or 1 in 25, but seems to have levelled off practically to zero when the river's edge was reached. In 1941 the water level in the Wye stood at 578 feet or 5 feet lower than the lowest point in the moat. Measurements indicate that if there were to be any water at all in the moat system, the river level would have to be at least 6 feet higher than in 1941. One foot of water in the middle basin would float a canoe; and for this to come about, the river level would have to rise 7 feet. A rise of 10 feet would flood the moat to a depth of 3 feet near the eastern terminus and bring the water table to within 1 foot of the surface.

II. THE WEST MOAT

One of the very noticeable features of the unexcavated site was an open ditch or moat which lay parallel with and close to the west side of the ruins beginning immediately south of the northwest bastion. It was about 6 feet wide and, on the average, 3 feet deep. At the south end of the Residence it turned westward and was lost under the driveway. The presumption is that after running west for a matter of probably 6 or 8 feet it again turned south and continued in that direction until it joined the main moat. This was, however, not proved, because of the existence of the modern driveway whose course coincides with the supposed course of the ditch (Map 8, X).

During the centuries much silt and débris accumulated in the channel. At one place, immediately west of the point where the Residence and Chapel met, it lost definition entirely. A large tree grew on the spot making observation impossible. There is no doubt, however, that the moat was either interrupted entirely at this point or made a short detour to the west.

The channel presented a number of interesting facts of minor importance. In that part which paralleled the Chapel, numerous fragments of charred boards lay on the bottom and on the east slope, quite without arrangement, as if they had fallen there. Large patches of charcoal were conspicuous elsewhere along the bottom of this segment, as well as mixed patches of charcoal, burnt clay, and clay, while at the roots of the tree there was a cache of charred corms, thought to be onions. The northern part of the south segment was remarkable for the number of loose stones which it contained. Some of these appeared to have come from a chimney fall, particularly those opposite the fireplace, but those farther south could not be accounted for so easily. They may conceivably have been left over from building operations, and never removed from the ditch. There were numerous charred boards in a very fragile condition in this segment, practically all of them lying lengthwise of the ditch. Their presence was obviously due to the fact that the walls of the Residence fell outwards.

The cross-section of the moat was fairly consistent throughout. For descriptive purposes the portion at 67J[1] will serve. At this point the maximum width was 7 feet and the depth 3 feet. One and one-half feet of modern humus overlay a shallow stratum of charcoal. Beneath the charcoal was a layer of sand not apparently water-laid, and beneath this again, on the eastern slope, an inch or two inches of burnt clay. This brick-like material rested on a clay subsoil. The charcoal and the burnt wood found elsewhere in the ditch came from the two adjacent buildings. The sand was probably washed in from the sides soon after the opening of the ditch. The burnt clay seemed to be present over most of the bottom of the ditch and especially at its southern end. It could not have derived from the buildings, since it is overlaid with sand; presumably, therefore, it was caused by the sun baking the exposed subsoil when the ditch was new.

The few specimens yielded by the moat included the charred corms above referred to, and the charred textile described on pp. 159-60, part of which was in the side of the moat and part on the sill of the Residence.

The supposition is that this feature linked up with the main moat near where the driveway crossed the latter. Since there is no evidence of silting, however, the connection between the two must have been of short duration. The ditch could have had very little protective value.

(d) Soil Stain Pattern

In numerous instances where excavation was carried down to otherwise undisturbed levels, distinctive markings appeared in the soil. Usually they stood forth conspicuously as dark bands of fill (humus, clay, red sand) in white sand. Frequently they were interrupted by the digging which had been done in erecting some of the buildings, but they generally resumed again and could be traced beyond the present structures. In the case of the southeast bastion, for instance, (the west and south walls), one of these bands diagonally crossed the west and south walls and continued beyond in both directions; west of the northeast bastion similar fills occurred, and these continued north beyond the curtain. There were others again in the field west of the compound, which were traced to show that they connected up with certain others in the south end of the enclosure.

While only a few of these fills were studied in detail, enough is known to say that they were as much as 1 foot across and extended for 2½ feet below the surface. The composition of the material shows that they were dug trenches, filled in with dirt containing such débris as burnt clay, ash, wood charcoal, some mortar, and occasionally even small bones, but never anything of importance. The trenches were generally uniform in width and straight throughout their length. The dark coloration suggested, though it did not prove, that the trenches once held wooden timbers (Map 10; Pl. xxɪɪ b).

Since many of these soil markings were interrupted by such structures as bastion walls, it seems clear that they antedated the latter. Unfortunately, not a great deal more can be said about their purpose, for their overall pattern was by no means complete, and that portion of it which did exist was confused. For instance, in the region between the two south bastions numerous trench fills occurred, crossing each other, for the most part at right angles, to make small enclosures, and then continuing in straight lines (Pl. xxɪɪ a). But if the rectangles so formed indicated rooms, they were very small indeed, and the purpose of the continuing lines still remains in question. The most reasonable supposition is that they represent the foundations of buildings earlier than the final ones; that the arrangement of these was changed from time to time, resulting in the confused pattern; and that the record of the markings is now incomplete. The same holds true for a row of small post- or stake-moulds running east from the sill in the Residence, crossing the great fireplace, and continuing some distance east of it, and for other arrangements of stake-moulds south of that structure, as may be seen on Map 10.

III. Specimens

THE long list of specimens contains objects of both Indian and European origin. A few Indian objects, such as a stone axe and broken pots, were found near the surface where they had been dropped or left after the destruction of the fort. Other specimens of the same origin lay mingled with European goods in close association, for example, the cloth which rested on the sill. Still others were seemingly contemporaneous with the European occupation but less closely associated. There was none that could be positively identified as antedating the erection of the Residence. The European remains were extensive, widely diversified, and in varying states of preservation, some being indifferently and some well preserved. All those which concern this Report are of seventeenth-century origin; those which date from the era of settlement are, with one or two exceptions, of little or no interest. A few specimens, however, are of indeterminate origin; they may date either from the seventeenth or nineteenth centuries and therefore must be mentioned in the description of European material.

Of the 40,000 specimens recorded, probably only one-tenth have historical or scientific interest; the rest were saved by virtue of their association with the site. For instance, in the course of most excavations of this sort, one or two samples of brick and mortar would be preserved; here, however, as before mentioned, considerable quantities were preserved, as well as all scraps of metal that could be found. The case with charcoal was somewhat different. Large pieces of it may be useful in establishing a tree-ring chronology for Ontario and the eastern woodlands generally, and were saved to that end.

The European objects throw a flood of light upon the life at Ste Marie in the days of the Jesuits and the Hurons. Many more specimens would have been found had not the retiring missionaries taken with them to Christian Island such goods as they needed and could carry; however, large numbers of broken, discarded, lost, or forgotten objects lay buried in the ruins, awaiting the excavator's shovel, and now are available for study. They are mute evidence of a brave attempt to plant in Huronia Christianity and the culture of France. They are also evidence of the kind of material equipment which we may assume was characteristic of New France at that period; and such evidence is, to say the least, scarce. We are especially fortunate in having recovered a wide range of tools which were used at the time by carpenters, masons, gardeners, and woodsmen. Numerous gun parts testify to the popularity of this important new weapon along the frontier of the then known world. Glass was a rare material, obviously highly prized and rarely used. Most of the kitchen crockery was probably taken away at the time of the exodus, but a few broken pieces reveal its one-time presence. Mute testimony of the arduous labour which was poured into the erection of the buildings is to be seen in the scraps of metal which fell discarded from the smith's anvil. Add to this the considerable number of nails and spikes gleaned from the site, and the collection of European goods will no doubt prove to contain the greatest number and most diversified assortment of iron tools and hardware ever to be recovered from a site of French occupation in the New World. Besides this distinction, it contains at least one splendid example of Venetian art, perhaps the first specimen of high artistic merit to be brought to America north of Mexico (frontispiece).

The contribution of the excavation to our knowledge of Huron culture is no greater than the history of the site, as told in the *Jesuit Relations*, would lead one to expect. That is to say, the site yielded a fair number of specimens of Huron origin, evidently mostly contemporaneous as might be expected from the purposes and uses of the establishment; but no Indian village or refuse deposits beneath or near it. This again conforms to historical evidence, for the *Relations* make it plain that the absence of Indian villages from the immediate vicinity was one of the main reasons for selecting this particular spot. However, small quantities of various Huron objects—pottery, horn and stone artifacts—were recovered and, as these are of known date, should provide a sound starting point for further studies in the region.

Trade goods, i.e. European artifacts, particularly weapons and ornaments, brought out for exchange with the Indians, shed considerable light on a rather obscure subject. It has long been known, of course, that the Indian trade was considerable, and that it included iron axes, "tomahawks," beads, and kettles, for these articles have been recovered in quantity from innumerable sites. But the exact style in use at any given period has been a moot question. Now, at least for the decade 1639-49, the fashion in these things is definitely established.

Some evidence about the food of the Jesuits and Hurons has likewise come to light. As yet, not all of it has been examined; the bones particularly are still unidentified, and consequently no detailed information about meat and fish foods can be provided other than that mammals, birds, and fish were used in quantity. The proportions in which these remains are due to Indians and to Frenchmen is also unknown. But proof that certain plants were utilized is at hand; corn, squash, and other remains are abundant. A few corms, thought to be onions, are the only evidence for the cultivation of Old World plants at Ste Marie.

Specimens of European Origin

(a) Metal

Among the thousands of metal objects are many whose use can be identified, such as nails, hinges, axes, and files. Perhaps these will constitute the most interesting part of the collection for many readers. Besides these, however, are numerous specimens which cannot be identified. Some have undergone so much alteration during the course of years, and particularly at the time of the destruction of Ste Marie, that it is now impossible to tell for what they were originally used. Others again, and these are the most interesting in certain respects, seem not to have been altered from their original form during the years, and yet cannot be assigned any specific use. Perhaps many of them were made on the spot to meet the needs of the moment. Analogies from modern life are abundant. Just as we today improvise little "gadgets" for temporary needs and discard them tomorrow for better or more standard objects, so we may be sure the French occupants of Ste Marie three hundred years ago were forced by circumstance to improvise many a little gadget to help them in emergencies, to eke out the scarcity of metal, or to feel out means of meeting new needs. When such objects are described in the text, an effort is made to suggest uses, but such suggestions are merely guesses. Doubtless some of the uses to which these objects were put will become more apparent in time, but for the present we can only submit the ideas which have come to us in the course of their examination, or through the kind suggestions of others who have seen them.

OBJECTS MADE OF IRON

I. CONSTRUCTION HARDWARE

Nails (Pl. xxx). Nails constituted one of the largest groups of specimens recovered from the excavations. This is, of course, as one would expect, for the main buildings of the Residence were of wood, and in the seventeenth century as today, iron nails were extensively employed in construction. Then, too, furniture, boxes, and other wooden equipment required the use of nails. Besides the nails of ancient origin, however, modern specimens were found, deriving more from refuse thrown on the site than from actual building operations, although certainly some of them may so be accounted for. Whereas nails of seventeenth-century origin were all hand-made, those of the nineteenth century were almost entirely machine products, either wire or edge-grip. Consequently it is an easy matter to distinguish the new from the old.

The nails dating from the Jesuit period of occupation were iron, except for one or two specimens of copper. The shaft was usually square in section, varying in length from a half-inch to 8 inches. Standardization of equipment was unknown in the seventeenth century; consequently nails cannot be neatly sorted as to size. If one allows for slight variations, however, the following classification can be established with the number of each kind shown below:

½	1	1½	2	2½	3	3½	4	4½	5	5½	6	6½	7	8	TOTAL
29	123	206	287	213	209	181	51	29	16	6	8	4	5	1	1368

The heads varied more in form than did the shafts. No device for heading nails was identifiable in the mass of material found, but it is most likely that a tool of one or other of the types shown by Mercer was employed.[*] The type of head common on the Ste Marie nails was flat, but some were convex on top and round or square in outlines, while a few were more or less pyramidal. A good many were rectangular in outline or too irregular to be classifiable. A somewhat rare form was that shown in Pl. xxx, Q, and Pl. xxxi, A, C, and E, in which the head was T-shaped. Mercer asserts such nails were used in floors because the head could be counter-sunk. The medium-sized nails were very likely used in ordinary construction work; the smaller ones for fine work on boxes and furniture. Fancy-headed nails like Pl. xxx, P, were doubtless ornamental, being appropriate for chairbacks and the like.

A group of seven 4½ inch nails with large convex heads had apparently all been driven into the same piece of wood and clinched on the back. They too were likely ornamental. Most of them came from the second level of 87Q[1]; the others from nearby squares.

From the clinching on this group, it is evident that they were driven into a 2½ inch thickness of wood. Other nails scattered over the site bore evidence of having been driven into wood of the following inches thickness: ⅝, 1, 1¼, 1½, 1¾, 2⅛, 2¼, and 2½. In several instances nails still had wood adhering to them; and nails driven into brass strips or plates were not uncommon. One round nail found in apparently undisturbed soil seemed to date from the seventeenth century.

Spikes and Spike Heads (Pl. xxxi). If an acceptable definition of a spike is "heavy nail five inches or more in length," the excavation yielded about three dozen, which were included in the tabulation shown on page 92. These varied in shape just as did the nails, although shafts were more frequently rectangular or chisel-shaped. In five cases, the heads were T-shaped; in eleven, they were pyramidal (Pl. xxxi, C). Numerous headless nails and a few headless spikes like those shown in Pl. xxxi, K and M, were found, and conversely, there were many heads of spikes. For some reason, these detached heads were frequently larger than any still remaining on even the largest spikes (Pl. xxxi, H, J, L). Most of the fourteen large heads were found north and east of the east portal; the rest south of the Residence.

[*]H. C. Mercer, *Ancient Carpenters' Tools* (Doylestown, Pa., 1929), figs. 202-3.

Ornamental Nails (Pl. xxxii). Three nails with ornamental heads were illustrated in Pl. xxxii, A, B, and C. One, (A), had an octagonal bulb near the end of the shaft, with paired volutes at top and bottom. It is 2⅝ inches long; the shaft was oval in section near the top, but became chisel-shaped at the bottom. Another, (B), had a small bulbous head set off from the shaft by a collar; while a third, (D), was roughly pyramidal on top, square-sided with flattened corners, and had a diameter of three-quarters of an inch.

Screw Nails and Threaded Nails (Pl. xxxii). A small number of true screw nails and other nails with threaded shafts was found. Of the first class, there were nine examples, all but one from the area south of the Residence, and one from the northwest bastion. These true screw nails had round shafts, threaded for all or part of their length from the lower end upwards, and grooved heads. On some the thread was much deeper than on others. The heads were oblong, with grooves three-quarters of an inch deep. In Pl. xxxii examples are shown at (E), (G), (J), (K), and (L).

Five headless shafts were likewise threaded for all, or part of their length (Pl. xxxii, F). Some of them were round, some square in section; but regardless of shape, they were threaded. Probably here, as in so many other instances, force of circumstance obliged the dwellers at Ste Marie to use expedients which they would not have had to adopt if material, time, and help had been more adequate. A stout nail with a wedge-shaped head (Pl. xxxii, H) must have been inserted, like all the others, into a started hole, but unlike them, turned with a pair of pliers.

Screw nails were used at Ste Marie, as elsewhere, in wooden construction. The use of threaded shafts is not so certain; perhaps some of those found were merely broken screw nails; others certainly were not. The only one found *in situ* was inserted through a hole in a concave iron disk; this same disk had five or six other ordinary nails in it as well, showing that it had been nailed to some wooden object (Pl. xxxvii). The mechanic had obviously run short of the usual material and used what lay at hand, a threaded nail originally intended for some other purpose.

Perforated Spikes (Pl. xxxiii). Three large spike-like objects had a perforation either rectangular or round at one end, as if they had been inserted through a slot or hole, or even a timber, and caught with a drop-key (Pl. xxxiii, B, C). They ranged in size from 3¼ inches to 5½ inches.

Staple (Pl. xxxiii). One U-shaped staple closely resembled its modern descendant, except that it showed plainly its hand-wrought origin (Pl. xxxiii, G).

Clamps (Pl. xxxiv; Fig. 14). Thirteen iron clamps, including five complete specimens, were recovered from the site. Eleven of these were flat strips the ends of which had been sharpened and bent parallel to form a U-shaped object; the remaining two were square in section. The largest specimen had two nail holes in the cross-bar section. They varied considerably in size and shape. In one case the cross-bar was ornamented with widely-spaced, transverse hatching. Widely distributed over the site were found three complete clamps within the area of the Residence, four fragments and one complete specimen south of it, three fragments along the west side of the compound, a complete one at the east end of the moat, and one fragment near the well (Pl. xxxiv, C-H). The specimen shown in Fig. 14, A, was ornamented with hatching.

Angle-Irons. Under this term are included all L-shaped iron objects, large and small, having one or both ends pointed. In some instances the end of an arm turned up in a hook; in others one arm might be three times as long as the other. Eight specimens were probably door-swings, for the short arm was round in section, the other pointed, and their weight was sufficient for such a purpose (Pl. xxxv, D, J, M-Q). Most of these swings were found near the Residence and the Chapel.

Six almost identical specimens, in which the arms were very short, were found in position in the sill of the Residence in Square 69K^1, where they had been used to splice two timbers (Pl. xxiv *a*). Had they not been found in position, their use might have been less certain. Two are shown in Pl. xxxiv, A-B.

Of the total twenty-nine specimens of angle-irons, 27 per cent were in the K^1 squares, 24 per cent in the M^1 squares, and 24 per cent in the area between the refuse pit and the large fireplace.

Tenons. Ten narrow iron bars from 4¼ inches to 5¾ inches long, rectangular in section, tapering toward one end, and slightly curved lengthwise, are here described as tenons, for lack of a

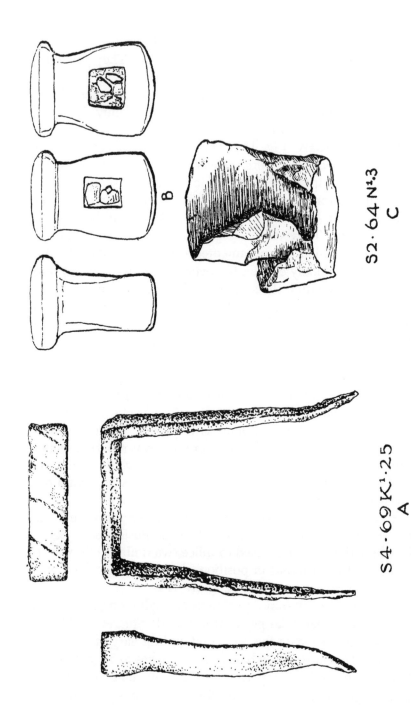

S2·64 N.º3
C

S4·69 K¹·25
A

B

Fig. 14. Iron hammer, ornamental clamp, iron ferrule. Scale: 1:1, except B, 1:2.

more accurate term. Two had a short reverse hook at one end. One specimen, 7¼ inches long, was, however, nearly straight and resembled a flat file in appearance. It was found in the root cellar. The tenth piece, found in 54Y¹, was split at one end. Another specimen split at the end is not included in the above count. Five of these objects, all very much alike, were found in 73O¹; the rest were widely scattered in 54Y¹, 60M¹, 64R¹, 73K¹, and 85S¹. All lay in or near wooden constructions.

Hooks (Fig. 15). Hooks found on the site showed a wide variety of form. One type was made by looping one end of a flat strip of iron and hooking up the other (Fig. 15, A). In a second type one end was bent upwards, the other sideways (C). The most usual form was that which was primarily U-shaped, but in which both ends bent in the same direction and at right angles to the arms of the U (B). A simple type was merely L-shaped or had the hook end slightly up-curved. Most of these could have been used for supporting objects of considerable weight.

Specimens of slender construction were probably used as clothes-hooks. A T-shaped example, found in 62R¹, was 4 inches long, up-curved at the long end, and perforated in the branches, and was not unlike a modern hat hook. A spike-like hook (Cat. S4-73K¹-29) was 4¾ inches long.

Small hooks from 1¼ inches to 2⅜ inches long were of various shapes; of these the most interesting perhaps was that which was shaped almost like a figure eight and retained a two-inch nail in the loop.

Eighteen objects could be identified as hooks; other small fragments in the collection were doubtless parts of hooks.

Hinges (Fig. 16). Including fragmentary and a few problematical specimens, there were at least twenty-two hinges found on the excavation. Some were plain and business-like and others elaborate and ornamental. Most of them may well have been made on the spot, but one or two at least, to judge by the fineness of workmanship, seem to have been imported. Not all were of iron; those of better quality were made of brass. Both strap and butt hinges were well represented, the latter being slightly in the majority.

For the most part strap hinges were rather rudely made. They

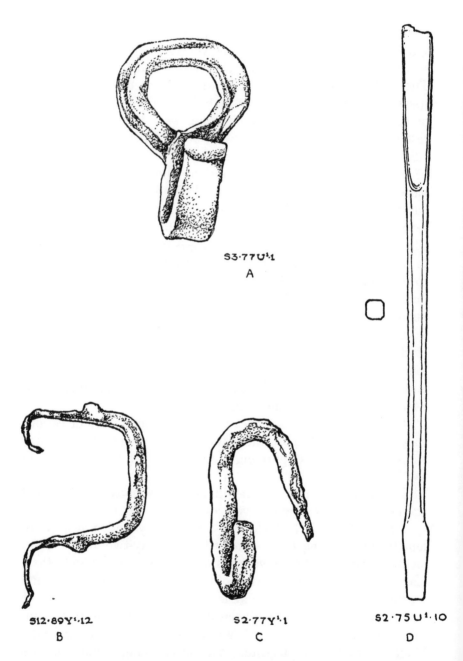

S3·77U¹·1
A

512·89Y¹·12
B

S2·77Y¹·1
C

S2·75U¹·10
D

FIG. 15. Iron reamer and hooks. Scale: 1:1, except D, 1:2.

were narrow triangles of metal, of which all or part of the larger end was bent over to form a socket. One, two, or three nail holes were punched at various distances along the blade. The longest specimen was 7¾ inches (Fig. 16, J). Another form of strap hinge had a spike at right-angles to the blade but in the same plane, for insertion into a socket attached to the frame (A). An exceedingly slender strap hinge was shown in the same Fig. at (C). Two diminutive brass hinges (G, K) were particularly well made, probably imported; one of them bore two rows of an embossed design. They were suitable for use on small boxes.

Eleven specimens of butt hinges were found, of which five were brass. Examples may be seen in Fig. 16, B, D, F, H, from which the range in size and form is evident. At (B) is one-half of an ornamental iron hinge with a thrice-scalloped edge; two other halves of the same style were also found. It is interesting to observe that two butt hinges were discovered just outside the northeast corner of the central fireplace, along with a concave iron disk (described below) and other metal ware.

Masonry Anchors (Pl. xxxvi). Three iron implements were so shaped as to indicate that they may have been embedded in masonry for use as anchors. One of these was a heavy Y-shaped object, with a large perforation at the solid end. Its length is 8½ inches (Pl. xxxvi, E). Another was approximately rectangular and originally had a square perforation at one end which occupied nearly half the entire area but is now broken (F). A third implement somewhat resembled a closed clevis, being a closed U, the flat end of which was slit. Its dimensions were 6 inches by 2¾ inches (H).

Heavy Perforated Irons. Plates xxxvi and xlv illustrate a number of iron objects with perforations. Those in Plate xxxvi, (A), (B), (D), and (G) were sturdily made as if for heavy use. (A) resembled a screw nut but was not threaded. One surface was flat and the other convex. (D) may have been the head of a heavy bar for a gate, the perforation allowing a key-pin to be inserted. The axe-like object at (G) in the same plate was an inch thick at the centre, but tapered to a thin edge at each end. In Plate xlv, (A) and (K) were similar, being flat, trapezoidal objects with a row of perforations. It is, of course, impossible to know if such things were for building or for other purposes.

Perforated Iron Straps (Pl. xlvi). An iron strap with a long rectangular perforation in the middle could well have been part of a door latch or hasp (Pl. xlvi, D). The Royal Ontario Museum collections contain a similar object said to have been found at Ste Marie. Another narrow strip, unperforated except for a pair of small nail-holes in the expanded head at each end, was found in an undisturbed area in 63L[1]. Six other pieces of strapping consisted of strips about 1¼ inches wide with nail holes at intervals. Three pieces were found in the Residence area, and one immediately west of the east curtain, north of the portal. This latter piece was interesting in having two "bites" out of one side and a group of three nail-holes at both ends. The largest piece found was 7½ inches long.

Nine fragments of sheet iron, all from the vicinity of the forge flue except one from 83Y[1] and another from 62H[2], were evidently made by cutting semi-circles from rectangles. The remainder left after this procedure had a rectangular outline with a large semi-circular "bite" from one long side (Pl. xlv, C. E). The dimensions of the best-preserved piece were 4½ inches by 2½ inches.

Circular Iron Objects, Perforated and Unperforated. A circular sheet of iron, 5⅜ inches in diameter, had numerous large perforations apparently made with square nails. A fragment of a similar piece lay in 62K[1]. Two unperforated specimens may have been originally parts of shovel blades. Their use, whether constructional or otherwise, is unknown.

Concave Iron Disks (Pl. xxxvii). Four concave iron disks, three of which were circular in outline and the fourth approximately rectangular, were found (Pl. xxxvii). Presumably they were used in the buildings in some way. One specimen lay along with four iron axes on the floor of the Residence at its northwest corner. Almost hemispherical in shape, it had four nail holes but no nails and was about 7 inches in diameter. A second, which was roughly rectangular in outline, lay just beyond the central fireplace, in association with hinges, boards, and other material which suggested some kind of box or cupboard. This specimen was 6½ inches long and 5¾ inches wide. Around its edge were eight nail holes with six 2¼ inch nails still in place; they were inserted from the concave side, as indeed they were

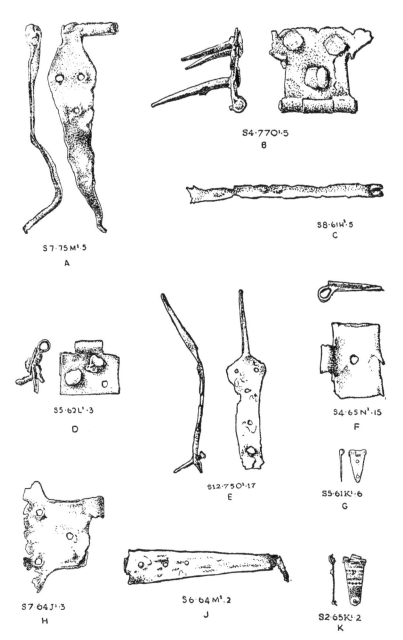

Fig. 16. Hinges of iron and brass. Scale: approximately 1:2, except E and J, 1:4.

in every case. A nearly circular disk 6 inches in diameter was discovered in 83U[1], which is immediately west of the turn in the east curtain. It was partially split. Five nails remained in place and two were missing. The fourth disk, S5-87S[1]-2 was found inside the north curtain in the line of the ditch. It was also nearly circular, with a diameter of 7 inches. Five of the eight nail holes still contained nails, one of which was partially threaded and had a cross-shaped slot in the head. It was much mutilated, however; the lower end had been split and flattened. The function of these objects is quite unknown. No two were identical; yet their appearance was sufficiently alike in all cases to lead one to think they all had had the same function, whatever it may have been. They seemed not to have been carefully fashioned; even allowing for the fact that they suffered from corrosion, their outlines were rough, the nail holes were irregularly spaced and uneven in size, and nails of several types were employed. There is no indication that they were subjected to heavy wear, despite the fact that they were so securely nailed. They may have had a structural function, or they may have been used as mortars for grinding corn, as Father Desjardin has suggested, or as patches according to the conjecture of Dr. H. A. Thompson.

Draw-Bar (Pl. xxix). A heavy bar of iron with a flattened, triangular head must have been a draw-bar device for tightening and holding some part of the wooden construction. It was 10 inches long, with a slot at the opposite end from the head, through which was driven a sturdy wedge 4 inches long. Sliding free between the wedge and the head was a stout iron washer 1½ inches in diameter and one-quarter of an inch thick (Pl. xxix, *b*).

Latches (Pls. xxxviii, xlvi). There were three iron objects which somewhat resembled latches. A flat bar was so cut as to leave a triangular projection along one edge near the middle, and the part beyond the projection was then bent backward. Two specimens were found within the Residence in 75K[1], and one in 64M[1]. The length of the longest was 5½ inches. Another specimen had the part beyond the triangular projection bent downwards instead of backwards. An anomalous specimen shaped like the three first described was bent double and was nailed from both sides with 4-inch nails (Pl. xlvi, A).

Three specimens which may have been latch-drops are shown

in Pl. xxxviii, E, G, and J. They consisted of a stem tapering to a point and a flat, triangular head in the same plane as one of the narrow sides of the stem. The head had either one or two perforations. If the suggestion already made is correct, these objects, combined with those described in the last paragraph, comprised handy door-catches. The first-described part was attached to the door frame in such a way that the triangular section protruded beyond it. The other part, the latch drop, was passed through a hole in the door so that it would, on being depressed from one side, raise a bar on the other which was caught against the triangular projection on the frame and so allowed the door to be opened.

Rings and Washers (Pl. xxxviii). Fifteen complete and fragmentary rings and washers were discovered, all but four of which lay between the Residence and the southwest bastion. Two, and possibly three, seemed to be modern. Some of the broken specimens may have been the end-loops of iron ladles, others broken links. The example shown at (A) in Pl. xxxviii was well made and square in section. An eye with a ring passing through it, in the manner of a modern hitching-post ring, was shown on the same plate at (H). Diameters vary from 1 to 2¼ inches.

II. BUILDING TOOLS

An interesting collection of tools was obtained on the site, much of which was in a good state of preservation. The use of a large proportion of the tools can be established, but that of some is problematical. As is natural, the larger tools were much better preserved than the smaller, more fragile ones.

Hammer (Fig. 14). An iron hammer head lay in square 61M[1], along with eight iron axes. When found, fragments of the wooden handle were still in place in the socket, with a nail driven in as a wedge. It was of a type best described as a smith's hammer, that is, it was rectangular in outline with a rectangular socket near the head end. The head was square with a convex surface and was separated from the body by a slight constriction; its dimensions were 2⅝ inches by 2 inches by 1 inch (Fig. 14, B).

Chisels (Pl. xxxiii). A large iron mortising-chisel, 9⅜ inches long, was well preserved, except that the head had been considerably damaged through use. The stout shaft which was rectangular in section was scarfed, or cut transversely, at the bottom. Near the head was a wide collar, above which the wooden handle originally was fitted (Pl. xxxiii, A).

Another chisel, seen in the same plate, was found in the first level, but appeared to be of seventeenth-century origin. It was 5⅝ inches long, square at the top, but becoming wedge-shaped at the bottom, with corners flattened off for easy gripping.

A third specimen, not illustrated, although it lacked a definite head and the lower part of it was bent, was probably a chisel. The wedge-shaped end appeared to have been used a good deal.

Punches (Pl. xxxiii). Five specimens, one of them fragmentary, may be included in this category. A bar, 8¾ inches long, square in section, and tapered to a very small blunt point appeared to have been used as a punch (Pl. xxxiii, F). Another punch, on which the corners had been flattened for easy gripping, was 6 inches long. The end, however, was damaged (Pl. xxxiii, D). Another specimen, 3 inches long, was probably modern.

Files (Pl. xxxix). Eight files, all different but all of undoubted seventeenth-century origin, were found (Pl. xxxix). One was discovered north of the central fireplace and another just west of the central ditch. All the others came from the area between the south end of the Residence and the southwest bastion. No matter what their form, they all showed unmistakably that they were hand-made tools, and even in their corroded and fragmentary condition indicated the skill which was employed in their fabrication. On the basis of Mercer's classification they may be divided into four types: two rat-tails, one half-round, four flat files, and one square file.

The two rat-tails (Pl. xxxix, F) were found in disturbed areas, but their type is a very ancient one and there can be little doubt that they date from the Jesuit period. One specimen showed much fine tooling.

The half-round file, seen at (B) in the plate, was plano-convex in section, and had the flat face tooled in two directions to mark it off into tiny diamonds. The convex face, assuming that the smaller was the upper end, had parallel grooves beginning at the left and running up to the right side. The workmanship was remarkably neat and accurate.

The square file was a heavy instrument, really rectangular in section rather than square, tapering at the far end to a sharp point (Pl. xxxix, H). All surfaces were coarsely cross-hatched with fairly wide grooves. The handle end was broken but the part which remained was 9¼ inches long.

The flat files may be subdivided into three types. The first of these was a fragment of a very thin tool, 1 inch wide. The grooving on it was fine but not always uniformly spaced. Moreover, one surface was entirely scored, the other only near the edge, at least as nearly as can be ascertained.

The second type of flat file was rectangular in section, tapered slightly toward the handle end, which was bent at a right angle, presumably for inserting into a wooden grip. Its surfaces were spirally grooved to the left as the tool was held in the hand, and one of the edges was also prepared for use (Pl. xxxix, A).

The last type is illustrated in the plate by two specimens, (C) and (G). They were thin rectangles in section and rectangular in outline, with tapering ends meant to be fitted into wooden handles. In (C), all surfaces were scored for use. The other specimen, found in square 57R¹, though crudely scored both as to depth and spacing was exceptionally interesting because it had the initials "IL" cut into the surface of one side. At least two men resident at Ste Marie bore names whose initials these may be. One was Fr. Jérôme Lalemant (in the seventeenth century "I" was used frequently for "J"), who lived there from 1638 to 1645, and the other the donné, Jacques Levrier, shoemaker to the establishment (1640-9). The servant Jean le Mercier may also be a claimant.

Screw-Driver (Pl. xl). Screw nails imply the use of screwdrivers, and while the tool seems rarely if ever to be mentioned until recent times, it did exist. Two tools found at Ste Marie can best be described as screw-drivers. One specimen, probably only fragmentary but still 1¾ inches long, had a round shaft, flattened from both sides at the end to form a straight bit. Irregular channels up each side and a round depression on the upper end of the bit-surface at one side suggest that it may have been a re-worked tool.

A fine specimen, shown in Plate xl at (A), is 7 inches long, had a sharp-pointed handle meant to be inserted into a wooden head,

and was square in section. There were faint indications that it
was grooved like a file.

Claws (Pl. XL). A series of six iron objects can only be described as claws. Three were square shafts flattened and curved
outward at the end and uncleft. The others had either a flat shaft
or a square shaft increasing in size at the far end, which was flattened and cut out to form a pair of claws. The impression is that
they were pulling tools for drawing nails or tacks (Pl. XL, B, C,
D, G).

Boring Tools. Reamers (Pl. XL): Those which we take to be
reamers were short, stout objects from 2 to 3¾ inches long with a
short, tapered handle, often set to one side of the longer end. The
blades were either square or rectangular in section and in four
cases slightly curved. The straight specimens particularly could
have served as reamers. They lay almost entirely between the
Residence and the southwest bastion (Pl. XL, E, H-L).

Gimlets (Fig. 17): Four fragmentary gimlets were recovered
in the same general region as the reamers. All except one had
flat rectangular heads, made to fit into a wooden handle or turning
lever, and a round shaft which for most of its length was channelled on one face. Consequently the working part was concavo-
convex in section. The exception had a broad head with three
perforations. The largest specimen was 5½ inches in its broken
condition. Perhaps a fifth specimen, very incomplete, should be
added to the above total. Two gimlets are shown in Fig. 17, A, G.

Another object possessing the same general characteristics except that the head was flattened and had three perforations was
found in 87U. Instead of being channelled only on one side, the
shaft here was channelled on both. The length was 5¼ inches.

Auger (Fig. 15): A large iron tool, 15½ inches in length, may
be more properly described as an auger or bit than as a gimlet
(Fig. 15, D). It closely resembled the specimens described under
that heading, except in the matters of size and sturdiness. The
head was wedge-shaped, about 1½ inches long and ⅞ inches wide
at the widest, tapering slightly at the end as if to fit into a wooden
cross-handle. The shaft, 8¾ inches long, was nearly uniform in
diameter throughout, and roughly octagonal in section. The boring
end was markedly concavo-convex in section, the outer edge

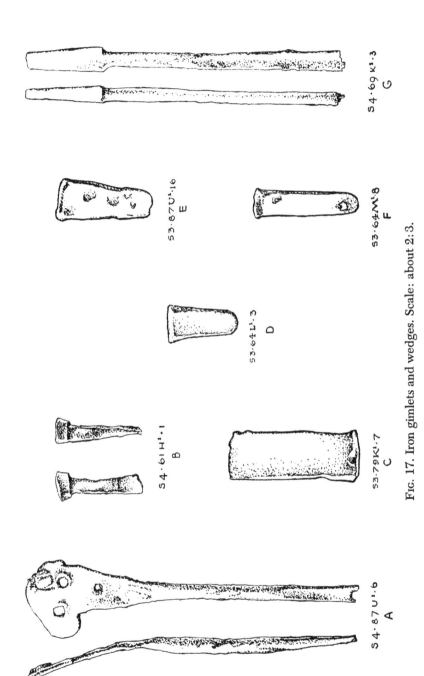

S4·87 U¹·6
A

S4·61 H¹·1
B

S3·79 K¹·7
C

S3·64 L¹·3
D

S3·87 U¹·16
E

S3·64 M¹·8
F

S4·69 K¹·3
G

Fig. 17. Iron gimlets and wedges. Scale: about 2:3.

strong and sharp for cutting. The end was closed and slightly enlarged.

Wedges (Pl. xxiv *b*; Fig. 17). The excavation of Ste Marie brought to light twenty-seven iron wedges, ranging in size from the large specimen found just outside the east curtain to diminutive ones of only an inch. Twenty-one were found in the area between the southwest bastion and the south end of the Residence, two inside the Residence, and two along the west side of the Chapel. The first group consisted only of small wedges such as might conveniently be used in taking up slack in joints of woodwork; the other groups were on the average somewhat larger (Fig. 17, B-F). The heavy wedge referred to above was a splitting tool which had received considerable hard use; it was 7¼ inches long and 2 inches wide (Pl. xxiv *b*).

Double-Pointed Bars (Pl. xli). Nine small bars were pointed at both ends, with points varying from dull to sharp. Five of these were square in section and had at the centre a collar or enlargement (Pl. xli, J-M).

Pike-Head (Pl. xxix *a*). A heavy object which may have been a pike-head was found in 79U¹, level 3. It will be seen from the illustration in Plate xxix *a*, that the specimen had a triangular head, flattened and flanged on two sides, and a long tapering shaft suitable for inserting into the end of a heavy wooden pole. Such a combination of wooden pole and iron head could be used as a crow-bar and would be far more economical of iron.

Trowel (Fig. 18). A large mason's trowel was uncovered in the stone-fall west of the east curtain. Made in one piece, it had a triangular blade 5¾ inches long and 3⅜ inches wide, and an L-shaped handle 6 inches long. The handle was placed asymmetrically on the blade and had a little curl at the end to give an additional grip to the wood in which it was encased (Fig. 18, A).

III. EDGED TOOLS

Relatively numerous were the specimens which may be included in this class, such as axes, knives, scalpels, and an adze.

Draw Shaves (Pl. xlii). One specimen, seen in Plate xlii, C, is thought to be a draw shave, although it may be considered by some to be part of a sword blade. It was a flat bar, 8¼ inches long

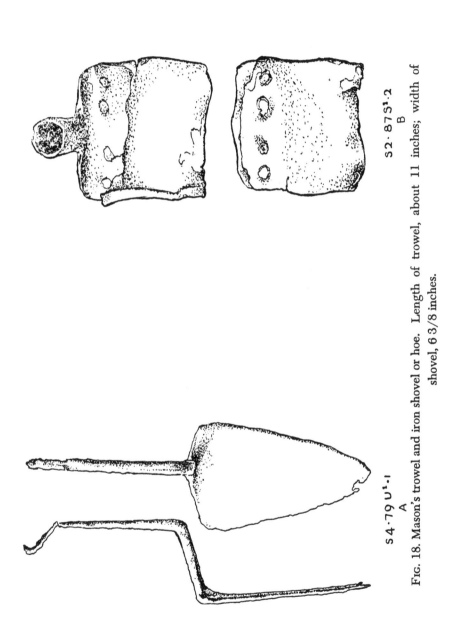

S4·79 U¹·I
A

S2·87S¹·2
B

Fıg. 18. Mason's trowel and iron shovel or hoe. Length of trowel, about 11 inches; width of shovel, 6 3/8 inches.

and 1 3/16 inches wide, slightly tapered at each end, but only along one edge. The tapered edge was sharpened for most of its length.

The specimen shown at A in the same plate was of indeterminate use and may be modern. It was thin, wide, and at the unbroken end oval. The upper edge was slightly thickened.

Knives (Pl. xlii). Seven knife-blades, more or less complete, and numerous fragments which presumably came from knives but were too small or too corroded to be identifiable are represented by the specimens shown in Plate xlii. The blades were very thin, tapered to a blunt point, and approximately 4 inches long and ¾ of an inch wide. In at least two cases they bore the vestiges of inscriptions or stamps on the left side, but none of the inscriptions has been deciphered.

In one case this more common style of blade was found with an unusual specimen. The latter had a blade of the usual type and part of an iron handle which must have been encased in bone or wood originally. It was exceptional, however, in having a raised collar between the two (Pl. xlii, D). Remains of rivets were evident in the handle.

There were two examples of short, sturdy knives with triangular blades which were relatively thick and unsharpened. The handles were only half the width of the blades, both of which were continuous along the back.

A small rectangular fragment with two small perforations at the large end had a square notch along one side, and may have been the end of a sword blade (Pl. xlii, G). Twenty-seven other small fragments were too incomplete to be identifiable, but probably half of them were parts of knife blades. Ten were found between the Residence and the southwest bastion, three inside the Residence, five in the northeast bastion, and the remainder inside the east and north curtains.

Scalpels (Pl. xli). A small scalpel with a blade 1 inch long was discovered in the sixth level of square 59J[1]. The blade was triangular in outline, the handle round, and the length 3¼ inches (Pl. xli, C). Another scalpel was 3¾ inches long and more elaborately made with a round shaft and a bulbous head. Ornamental raised rings marked the transition between shaft and head and between shaft and blade. The instrument was indeed sufficiently like the awl described on page 120 to be part of a set. The blade curved along the back and was about two-fifths of the total length of the instrument.

Hatchet (Pl. xl). An iron object somewhat resembling a small hatchet is illustrated in Plate xl, F. It had a long, wedge-shaped blade, the inside edge of which was concave, and a very blunt bit. The short head, probably broken, was narrower than the blade.

Adze (Pls. xxix, xlvi). One carpenter's adze was found on the site, very close to the exterior of the west wall of the Chapel. It was 8½ inches long and the widest part of the blade was 4¾ inches. It consisted, like the axes, of two parts, the socket and the blade. The socket was probably shaped around a handle form like the axes, for it was of similar construction; it covered 2½ inches of the handle and was circular in cross-section. The metal here was about 3/16 of an inch thick. After being lapped around the handle form, about one-half of the sheet of metal was cut away on what was to be the inside of the tool. The remainder was hammered out into one solid blade, greater hammering reducing the thickness and increasing the width towards the bit. The blade was therefore triangular in outline except for the slight convexity of the bit. The outer face of the blade was very slightly convex. Like the axes, this tool had no poll or counterweight, and its handle was straight (Pl. xlvi, H).

Axes (Pls. v, xliii, xliv). Thirty-eight axes excavated on the site were practically complete, while fourteen fragments were probably parts of axes. Only about sixteen were well enough preserved to be usable; the remainder of the complete axes had broken sockets or broken blades. The socket was missing entirely from twelve specimens and five had obviously been used as wedges, presumably by Indians. One specimen in particular showed rough usage of this sort (Pl. xliv, A), for it had been so battered that it had spread apart along the original line of welding. The blades were seldom sharp, often showing evidence of rough usage in nicks and curled-back edges. Since Europeans in the wilderness would prize their axes above most other possessions and take good care of them, the damage shown on so many specimens argues strongly for Indian use.

Although seventeenth-century axes were found in many parts of the site, even outside the fortified area, the majority of them were localized in three principal areas inside the compound. The most prolific was that between the Residence and the southwest bastion, particularly in squares 60M¹ and 61M¹. Apparently the workshop occupied these and adjacent squares, judging by the number of iron tools and the amount of scrap iron in the area. Eight axes, four of them in moderately good condition, lay in 60M¹ in a cluster as if they had fallen there from a bench or wall. Six more came from square 61M¹. Square 75K¹ yielded four almost perfectly preserved, while a badly battered one came from 75M¹. In square 73O¹, two well-preserved specimens were discovered, one of them particularly noteworthy for having about six inches of the charred wooden handle still in position in the socket. The specimen was probably new, since the blade showed no sign of use. It was still quite sharp and was unusual, moreover, in having a straight cutting edge or bit (Pl. v *b*). Four specimens, one of which lacked a socket, were recovered from the northeast bastion. A fragmentary socket was found near by, however. Other axes were found in various localities, such as 87O¹, 87U¹, 62O¹, 67O¹, and 63L¹.

When uncovered, all specimens were corroded to a greater or less degree. To halt this process of disintegration, the axes were electrolytically treated to remove the rust, then washed, dried, and finally thoroughly coated with beeswax. At the moment of writing, twenty-eight specimens have been so preserved. Besides stopping the progress of deterioration, the treatment in large measure reveals the original surfaces, so that in many cases it is possible to analyse trade or stamp marks and other characteristic features.

Where corrosion destroyed the original surface texture of the metal, it often reveals many structural details. For instance, it showed that to make an axe, a strip of metal was partially bent back upon itself to form a socket, and that the join was then made by hammering the ends together. The result was that the blade was made not of a solid piece but of the two welded ends. Sometimes this construction was vividly shown when the blade had split along the original join. Original striations of the metal were also clearly visible in corroded specimens, the striations always running lengthwise.

Trade Marks: It is well known that early iron axes dug up on Indian sites bear certain distinguishing marks, popularly called "fleurs-de-lis." They ordinarily consist of three small impressions, arranged in an equilateral triangle, made upon both faces of the blade just below the socket. Good examples may be seen in Plate XLIII A, C, and E and less clearly on other specimens shown on the same plate and in Plate XLIV. There were four axes, however, in which there was but one punch mark on each side, as shown in the last-mentioned plate at D. Being of only moderate depth as a rule, many of them have been obliterated by rust; this fate has overtaken at least six specimens.

The marks themselves appeared to have been made with a punch die; consequently the impressions vary a good deal in depth and in clarity, depending upon the condition of the die and the force of the blow struck. A study of the marks reveals that they varied in detail; the inference being that each maker had his own mark. It may be, however, that the individual maker used a mark controlled by the guild to which he belonged. At any rate the axes from Ste Marie bore eight, or possibly nine, distinct marks (see Fig. 19). For isolating these, there are but two criteria, design and diameter. The designs may, of course, vary considerably or may approximate each other so closely as to be almost indistinguishable. In such a case, they may sometimes be isolated on the basis of diameter of punch marks, since it would almost be beyond the bounds of probability that two punches used by the same smith would be identical.

These axes were indubitably of French manufacture, and the marks they bore were those of French artisans or guilds, as the case may be, of the seventeenth century. They conformed in shape to one general pattern, from which variations were insignificant and few. Size was more variable than shape, for the smallest in the collection was 6¼ inches long by 3 inches wide and the largest 8⅝ inches long by 3⅜ inches wide. Length-width ratios were not constant however; one specimen, only 7⅜ inches long, had a maximum width of 4¼ inches.

Compared with our modern axes in form, they differed in

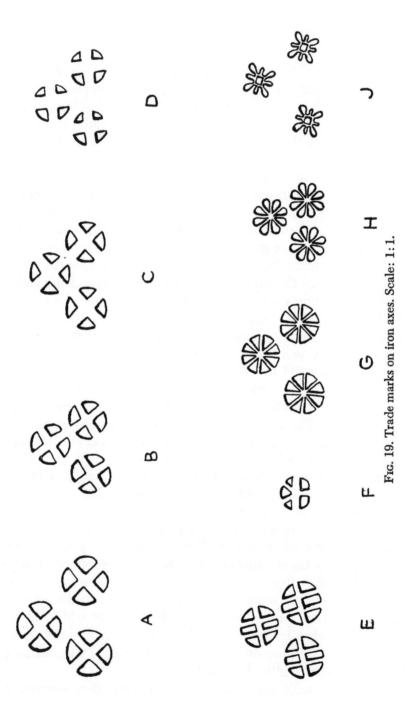

Fig. 19. Trade marks on iron axes. Scale: 1:1.

several important respects. Most important perhaps was the angle at which the handle was set. Whereas modern axes have curved handles and bits almost parallel to the back of the head, the product of France, and of Europe, in the seventeenth century, had a bit which curved upward and inward towards the handle, which in addition was straight. The tool must have been decidedly unwieldy compared with modern axes. Secondly, the socket in the trade axe was merely a thin loop of metal at the very top of the tool, providing no counterweight; the efficiency of modern axes is due, in no small measure, to the large and heavy head above the socket. Finally, in the old axes the far side of the blade was straight and nearly at right angles to the line of the handle, as against the concave sides found on most axes in use at present. Near the south end of the compound, a highly interesting specimen was found which well illustrates the transition between the two types, ancient and modern. It is shown at the left in Plate XXVIII *b*. In it, the counterweight was already present, and the bit angle had been decreased, but the far side was still nearly straight and the balance imperfect. The specimen appeared to be an early American axe, probably discarded by a nineteenth-century pioneer of the district.

Unidentifiable Edged Tools. Two fragments of heavy tools have not been identified. One of these resembled the upper part of an axe broken through the socket but differs from French trade axes of the period in having a rectangular head protruding well beyond the socket. The other specimen appeared to be part of the head of a similar object.

IV. GARDENING TOOLS

Mattock or Hoe (Pl. xxv *b*; Fig. 18, B). A kind of mattock or heavy hoe which lay in 87S[1] was particularly interesting for two reasons. First, it is probably a unique specimen so far as seventeenth-century Canada is concerned, and therefore reveals to us something of the methods used in preparing the virgin soil for cultivation. Secondly, its condition illumines the state of affairs at Ste Marie during the decade of its occupation. The object was made roughly from a heavy sheet of iron by bending it to the desired shape, as seen in Fig. 18, B, and then cutting and folding back part of the sheet to make the ferrule or handle-socket. The tool was broken and repaired, probably because it was more economical of metal to repair it than to make a new one. The repair was made by cutting a section of sheet iron and riveting it roughly with four rivets to the remaining part, and by folding the excess material along the right side. The socket was provided front and back with a large perforation for the reception of a nail or other securing device. The specimen was 6½ inches wide and the same in length. It was found close to the inside of the north curtain east of the ditch in the second level (Pl. xxv *b*).

Ferrules (Pl. xlv; Fig. 14). One of the largest groups of iron specimens consisted of ferrule-like objects. There was such a wide variation in their appearance that no hard and fast rule may be laid down to describe them, except that in general terms they consisted of a single piece of iron bent up at each edge and possessing, usually, a convex bit. In many cases, one gets the impression that the iron was wrapped around a round handle to form a ferrule, although others are too open to have been so used. One specimen (Cat. S3-61H¹-3) still had wood in place (Pl. xlv, F). A few of the wider, shallower objects included in this group may have been bits of hoes or other such tools which had been cut up and discarded. The average size was 1 inch by 1½ inches. Approximately eighty specimens should be included under this description, of which 66 were found in the area between the Residence and the southwest bastion, three in the region of the storage pit, five in or near the Residence, and the remainder chiefly in or near the northeast bastion. A small number of these objects is illustrated in Plate xlv at B, D, F, H, and J, and in Fig. 14, C.

V. HOUSEHOLD ARTICLES OF METAL

Iron Vessels (Pl. xlvi). Three small fragments of iron vessels were found. The largest was a heavy piece 4½ inches by 2¾ inches, presumably from a large cooking pot. A rim fragment of another vessel was thin and much corroded. A third piece came from the shoulder of a small pot, while a fourth retained a small loop lug (Pl. xlvi, B). A Y-shaped piece with a small perforation may also have been the lower portion of a handle attachment.

Handles for Vessels (Pl. xlvi). One complete and two fragmentary handles for pots are in the collection (Pl. xlvi, C and E). The complete specimen was a semi-circle of iron with a diameter of 4⅜ inches, flattened and perforated at each end. A large iron rivet was still in place. The larger of the incomplete pieces was merely an iron rod bent into a loop at the end, and the smaller fragment was similar to it. Two iron loops were conceivably the ends of other handles.

Iron Rods for Pot Rims (Pl. xlvi). Eighteen iron rods were longitudinally curved, suggesting that they were bands over which the rims of kettles or pots were folded and hammered. Lengths ranged from 1⅛ to 5¾ inches. Half of them were recovered between the Residence and the southwest bastion (Pl. xlvi, G).

Sieve. In the southwest corner of the northwest bastion, among ash and charcoal, there lay several fragments of iron sieve, the largest of which was 5 inches by 1¾ inches. Whether or not it had been designed for culinary use may never be known. It was, however, flat with rows of small perforations all punched from one side. The holes were uneven, as if made by hand with a nail, and approach no closer than ¼ inch to the rim, except that in each corner one perforation was punched from the reverse side.

Eating Forks (Pl. xli). A small two-pronged iron fork lay in the fourth level of square 73K^1, just outside the Residence wall. Its handle was round, tapering slightly toward the far end. The head was flattened, as if for the accommodation of an ornamental facing, and perforated with two small holes. The handle faintly showed a pair of encircling grooves. Its length was 3¾ inches. The straight tines were set at an angle of about 120° to the handle, which, to us, gave the fork the appearance of being most inconvenient to use. They were flat, tapered towards the end, and were set parallel to each other; their length was 1⅜ inches. Unfortunately, a large part of one tine was missing (Pl. xli, B).

A small and slender instrument, shown at (D) in the same plate, was found near the fork, and may possibly have been for table use also. One end was broken, but the portion which remained appeared to have been hinged at the centre, and the remaining arm was bent inward at the end. It may therefore have been used much as we use tongs. Its length was 3⅝ inches.

Sewing Equipment (Pls. XXXVI, XLI, XLVII; Fig. 20). Sewing Kit: Beneath the charred wood in square 87M[1] there lay the remains of a kit of instruments which must once have been the property of either the tailor or the infirmarian. A pair of scissors, a silver needle-case containing remains of three needles, a spatulate instrument, a tweezers-like instrument, and two plano-convex strips of iron, probably the fragments of an instrument similar to the last, constituted the outfit. The scissors were in a moderately good state of preservation, although they could not be opened, and were surprisingly modern in shape. They were a trifle more angular than ours, for the shanks were square in section. The finger and thumb holes were oval and of equal size, and the general appearance pleasing. The length was 5⅛ inches (Fig. 20, E). The needle-case was in perfect working condition. The little cap fitted perfectly and was fastened by giving a slight twist to the right. It was delicately embossed with an exquisitely chased design. The tubular part of the case terminated in a scarfed section, at the end of which was a ring. Therefore, the case itself must have served some purpose such as a holder for a hooking device, but the complementary part was not discovered (Fig. 20, A). Enclosed within the case were the fragmentary needles, one of which may be seen in Plate XLI, E. They had suffered severely from rust, so that only two retained the eye. They do not differ materially from modern needles except that they are somewhat heavier. The spatulate object may have served to hold open button-holes while they were being stitched; at least similar instruments called stilettos seem to have existed. It was 6⅛ inches long, triangular in the wider portions, but changing to flat in the narrower. The triangular portion was oblong in outline (Fig. 20, G). The tweezers-like instrument, seen in the same figure (C), was a round strip of iron which has been split lengthwise for half its length to produce a small gripping tool with a spring. Its present length is 4⅜ inches.

A thimble found in the top level of 99U was made of brass with a much-corroded sheeting of iron (Fig. 20, B), and is of indeterminate age.

In addition to the scissors of the tailor's kit, seven fragmentary specimens were found scattered over the site, principally between

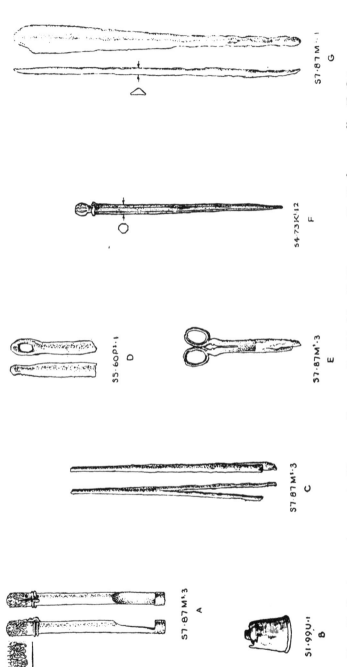

Fig. 20. Sewing equipment. A. Silver needle case; B. Thimble; C. Tweezers; D. Broken needle; E. Scissors; F. Awl; G. Stiletto. Scale: slightly less than 1:2, except E, which is about 1:4.

the Residence and the southwest bastion, with one in 75K[1]. Two fragments had the finger-hole intact; the rest were blades (Pl. xlvii, A-D).

Out of a total of seven needles, none was perfectly preserved. A moderately well-preserved one was 1⅝ inches long. The head of a very large needle may be seen in Fig. 20, D, the oval eye of which was 5/16 inches long, and the shaft round.

An awl, shown in Fig. 20, F, had a hexagonal shaft tapering to a moderately sharp point and a bulbous head. The latter was separated from the shaft by a small ring, just as was the case with the scalpel described on pages 110-11. Its length was 4⅜ inches; its provenance, square 73K[1], level 4.

Two pins made of a white metal were dropped at various times at the south side of the double fireplace in levels which had not been disturbed since Jesuit days. In these, the stem was about twice as stout as is the case in modern pins, and the head was a diminutive bulb. The length was 1¼ inches (Pl. xli, G, H).

A small number of iron hooks and eyes were found on the site. Four were inside the area of the Residence, one in the Chapel and two south of the Residence. They varied in length from ⅝ to 1¼ inches. To make them, a piece of iron wire was bent double and the ends given a double curve backwards, or else the bent end was curved downwards (Pl. xlvii, E-H).

Seven eyes or fragmentary eyes were recovered, all but one of which lay in the area between the Residence and the southwest bastion. The exception was found in 87Q[1], near the well. The three complete specimens were U-shaped, with the ends curved outward and downward to touch the sides (Pl. xlvii, J-M).

Locks and Keys (Pl. xlviii). The site yielded three padlocks, from 63J[1], 75M[1], and 83Y[1]. None, of course, was in working condition, notwithstanding the fact that all were moderately well preserved. They were all the same in shape, being equilateral triangles with semi-circular arms.

The largest specimen was 2¼ inches by 2⅛ inches with a thickness of 11/16 inches. The catch mechanism was rusted in an open position. It is not clear precisely how many parts comprised the lock and how they were put together. A raised edge encircled the body, however, and it appears that the two parts of the body were sprung together along this line. The keyhole was a narrow slit 9/16 inches long, and was surrounded by a rectangular chamber, no doubt provided originally with a cover to protect the mechanism from the weather. A narrow triangle of brass was inset into the centre of the reverse side and traces of brass sheeting were visible in several places elsewhere (Pl. xlviii, D).

The second lock, seen on the same plate at B, was intermediate in size between that just described and the next. Its width was 1¾ inches and its length 1⅝ inches. It was heavily corroded, the catch arm was lost, and one side was crushed in. It lacked both the keyhole shield and the brass sheeting.

The last and smallest lock was but 1⅛ inches wide, ⅞ inches long and ½ inch thick. Its arm was locked shut. The body was made of brass, unlike the others, though the arm was iron. The shield to the keyhole was a flat piece of brass which had become fixed with corrosion (Pl. xlviii, C).

Three keys were found, widely scattered over the site; two of them were in disturbed levels (Pl. xlviii, F, G). The specimen illustrated at F is a good example, and serves well for descriptive purposes. The head was ring-shaped and flat-sided, merely a flat strip of metal bent into a loop. The shaft was round. The flange or plate was cut more elaborately than that of a modern key. Two of those found showed traces of brass sheeting. Lengths vary from 1⅝ inches to 2⅝ inches.

A brass spigot with a head in the shape of a clover-leaf, each section of which had a large perforation, had a round shaft laterally perforated. Just above the shaft on one face of the head was a serpentine impression of two lines, probably a maker's mark. The specimen lay near the north curtain in a disturbed level. Its length was 2 inches.

Miscellaneous (Pl. xli, A). An iron cork-screw is shown on Plate xli, A, the shaft of which was round to irregular in section, and the end turned to a spiral and a half. The spiral may originally have been longer. The upper part of the shaft was much more corroded than the lower, which may be due to the presence of a wooden handle there. The length was 3½ inches. The specimen was found in 65K[1].

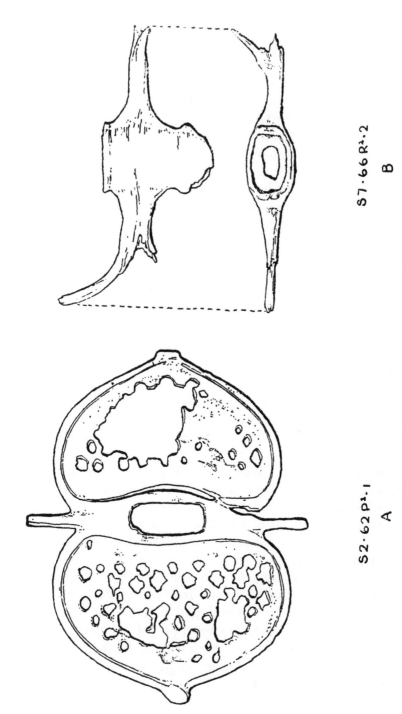

S2·62 P¹·1

A

S7·66 R¹·2

B

Fɪɢ. 21. Sword parts. Width of A, 4 3/8 inches.

VI. WEAPONS OF WAR AND OF THE CHASE

Sword Parts (Fig. 21). Two sword parts were uncovered; a guard in 62P[1] and a fragmentary hilt in 66R[1], probably both from the same weapon. The former was found in the second, the latter in the seventh level. The hilt fragment, shown in Fig. 21, B, was cross-shaped in outline with the arms of the cross bent inwards at the ends. The socket was oval. In this heavily corroded specimen the lamination of the metal is particularly noticeable; it runs the long way of the arms.

The guard had two convex, heart-shaped wings, one on either side of a central frame. The frame had a rectangular perforation for the adjusting of the handle of the blade. The wings were neatly perforated with rows of moderate-sized holes, edged with a solid, raised rim. Similar guards appear on swords of the early eighteenth century (Fig. 21, A).

Guns (Pls. xxxii, xlv, xlviii; Fig. 22). Numerous fragments of gun barrels and other gun parts came to light, some of them problematical, others obvious enough.

Parts of gun barrels: Fragments of heavy iron tubes were almost certainly pieces of exploded gun barrels. The interior was always round, but the exterior might be round or octagonal (Fig. 22, A). The specimen illustrated was threaded at one end. In several instances, the bore decreases slightly in size from one end to the other. In no case, however, was a complete section preserved; diameters are from ⅞ to 1¾ inches; and bores from ½ to 1¼ inches. Most of the specimens were found in the workshop area.

Gun springs: Fourteen specimens have been tentatively identified as springs, some of them gun springs. They were as a rule heavy bars of iron bent to a U-shape so that the inside faces were nearly in contact. They would be clumsy but powerful; yet similar ones may be seen on guns of the period (Pl. xlv, G).

Miscellaneous gun parts: At least thirty-three objects may well have been parts of guns, such as triggers, sears, flint-holders, and plates and mechanisms no longer used. Almost without exception they were found in the workshop and adjacent areas.

It would be tedious to the reader to have all these described, but several of the specimens illustrated may bear comment. For instance, on Plate xlviii the objects shown at (J-N), and (Q) were

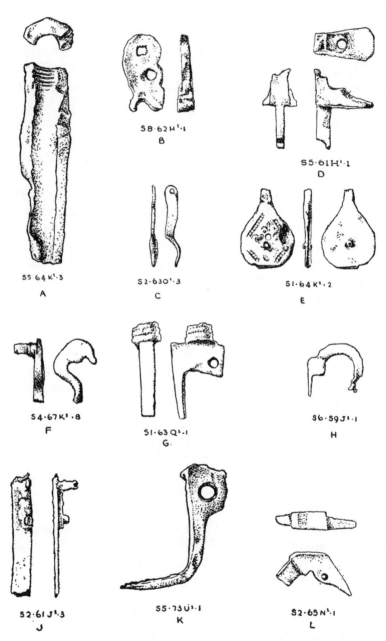

S8·62H¹·ı
B

S5·61H¹·1
D

S5 64 K¹·3
A

S2·630¹·3
C

S1·64K¹·2
E

S4·67K⁵·8
F

S1·63Q¹·ı
G·

S6·59J¹·ı
H

S2·61J¹·3
J

S5·73U¹·ı
K

S2·65N¹·ı
L

FIG. 22. Gun parts. A. Exploded barrel; C. Trigger; E. Cap; J. Plate, etc. Length of A, 4¼ inches. Scale of remainder, about 1:2.

likely gun mechanisms, while that at (O) was a brass trigger. (P) on the same plate was the upper part of a flint-holder from a flint-lock; a type of gun just coming into favour in Europe at the time.* Another part of a flint-lock, brass-plated, may be seen in Fig. 22, D. Various other gun parts are illustrated in Fig. 22, in which (C) is easily identified as a trigger. The cap at (E) was brass-plated and finely engraved on one side. In addition to the specimens referred to, it is likely that others described and illustrated elsewhere in this report may also have been used on guns, for example, the large, ornamental set-screws shown in Pl. xxxii, C, K, would be suitable for use with the flint-holders.

Balls (Pl. xlviii). Seven pieces of lead shot varied in diameter from ¼ to ⅝ inches, and in weight from 1.4 gms. to 27.1 gms. A larger iron ball, which was hollow and quite knobby on the surface, weighed 15.7 gms. and was 15/16 inches in diameter. It is shown on Pl. xlviii, R and two lead shots at (S) and (T). Lead shot was likely made on the spot, some of the smaller pieces possibly in a mould presented many years ago to the Royal Ontario Museum and said to have been picked up on the site of Ste Marie. Most of the balls still bear mould marks.

Ramrods (Pls. xlviii, l). Twelve objects were isolated as parts of ramrods, most of them tentatively, but the specimen shown at (E) in Plate xlviii was undoubtedly such. A similar object in brass indeed preserved part of the wooden rod to which it was attached (Pl.l, N).

Hunting Weapons (Pl. xlix). Points: Two iron and three brass points were recovered from the west side of the compound. They were all essentially of the same shape, that is, isosceles triangles with the corners sharply recessed. One of the brass points had a triangular tang, and one of the iron points originally had also. Lengths ranged from 1 to 1⅜ inches. Such points could without difficulty be affixed to wooden shafts. Their scarcity raises the question whether they were made as trade staples or as favours to Indians (Pl. xlix, D and E).

Fish-Hooks (Pl. xlix). While most of the fish-hooks were greatly damaged, barbs were still present on two (Pl. xlix, F, G).

---

*These pieces throw an interesting sidelight on the rapidity of diffusion, in that the flint-lock seems to have been invented just prior to 1630 and was not readily adopted in France (W. W. Greener, *The Gun and Its Development*, London, 1885).

Five barbless hooks may have been for fishing, but it is doubtful if the large one shown at (C) would be so used. One specimen showed a small perforation at the end, owing possibly to rust; otherwise the ends were generally flattened but unperforated. The ten hooks recovered were not localized in one spot, although three were from the workshop area, two from the storage pit, and three from the Residence floor.

Hunting or Fishing Weapons (Pl. xlix). Harpoons: Two long iron rods with triangular points which may be described as harpoons are illustrated in Plate xlix, A and B. Lengths were 7½ inches and 8¼ inches respectively; the shorter specimen had the larger head. One was found along the outside of the Chapel wall, the other north of the Chapel fireplace.

VII. MISCELLANEOUS IRON

Of the iron material not included in the foregoing analysis, most was unidentifiable. A few pieces, however, had definite form, a description of which may interest some readers.

Caps: Plate xxxviii, F, illustrates a small triangular piece of iron at one end of which is a downward hook. The object may have served as a cap of some sort on a mechanical contrivance.

Picket Tops: Four objects resembling tops of iron pickets were found in various squares, $60K^1$, $65J^1$, $65K^1$, and $77A^2$. The stems all seemed to be broken, so their original length cannot be estimated. Two had perforations near the large end (Pl. xxxviii, D).

Chain Links: Two sections of chain link, a large one probably modern, and a smaller apparently ancient, were unearthed in square $69K^1$. The large specimen is illustrated at (L) in Pl. xxxviii.

Wire: Four fragments of wire were found, none of them in locations which were positively undisturbed. One piece, however, was likely of seventeenth-century origin. This wire is drawn; confirmation of the existence of this technique of manufacture may be seen in the cloak hooks, also made of drawn wire.

Ingots: The rough ingot shown in Plate xxxvi, C, was but the largest of several discovered on the site. This specimen weighs about 3 pounds.

Bangle: Only one conical bangle with scalloped edges of a

sort popular with the Hurons was found on the site (Pl. xxxviii, K).

Bells: Two fragmentary iron bells found on the site were almost certainly for religious use and are described under section (f) of this chapter.

OBJECTS OF BRASS AND COPPER

The amount of brass was exceeded only by that of iron; the number of brass specimens made for some obvious purpose was however much smaller and consisted mainly of a few utilitarian objects like pegs and rivets and a small number of ornamental and miscellaneous goods. Among the brass objects were some of the most interesting specimens found on the site, including a coin, a fine instrument, and a bone object sheathed in copper.

Most of the 2,500 specimens were concentrated in the area of the workshop, although others were scattered widely over the site, especially inside the compound. Some of the brass objects, for instance a bell and numerous turnings of no real significance, were difficult to identify as seventeenth-century and are likely modern. Other material, again, of undoubted French origin, was apparently utilized by Indians who cut up sheets from kettles to make variously shaped fragments, mostly discards, but occasionally left a complete artifact.

I. HARDWARE

Hinges (Fig. 16). Four brass hinges were described under "Hinges" on pages 97, 99.

Rivets (Pl. l). Twenty-seven rivets retained the shaft and one head; two were complete with both heads. The largest rivet found had a head 1¼ inches in diameter, and a shaft 1 inch long; the average dimensions were about ⅝ inch and ½ inch respectively. A pair in place in a copper bar was found in 63M¹. The heads of nineteen other rivets were found; these were, on the average, somewhat larger than those above described (Pl. l, E, F, O, P, R, and S). Three copper slugs may be modern.

Pegs (Pl. l). Eleven pegs were made of copper by rolling the sheet metal and affixing a flat top of the same material (Pl. l, H-L). They were sturdy, and averaged about 1 inch in length.

Tubing. In twenty-seven cases, narrow strips or rather squares of heavy sheet brass were folded over to form a sort of tube, the edges being left untouched, resulting in an oval cross-section. One piece of tubing an inch long and particularly well made retained some vegetable fibre wrapping.

II. PARTS OF WEAPONS

Gun Parts (Fig. 22). A number of mechanical parts, some at least presumably from guns, were found. Most of these were referred to in the section dealing with guns (pp. 123-5), and a trigger is illustrated in Fig. 22, C.

Points (Pl. XLIX). Three brass points were described on page 125.

Ramrod Butts (Pls. XLVIII, L). One specimen of brass has been already described on page 125. A second ramrod butt appears to be of lead ensheathed in brass.

III. ORNAMENTS

Rosettes. A four-leafed copper rosette was slightly damaged. A leaf of a similar object was also found. Their use is unknown, but it is presumed they were for house or sanctuary adornment.

Pendants. A concavo-convex object appeared to be a pendant, with three small perforations at one end.

Bangles. Two slender cones of sheet brass were of a type of bangle popular with Huron Indians, and may have been made by them.

Cut-outs. A specimen made of sheet brass ¾ of an inch long was anchor-shaped, while another remotely resembled an animal form.

Ring. A crudely made copper ring found in 77M¹ had a small rectangular bezel upon which was a simple design somewhat resembling the letter E. The ring itself was plano-convex in section and hollow. Its diameter was 13/16 inch and its weight 1.4 gm.

IV. MISCELLANEOUS

Pin. A short, rather stout pin with a bulbous head lay in 79M¹, level 2. Its length was ¾ of an inch.

Tweezers. Two pairs of copper tweezers were recovered, the more finished one from the first level of 73Q¹, and the other from the ninth level of 75O¹. The first pair was 2⅜ inches long and

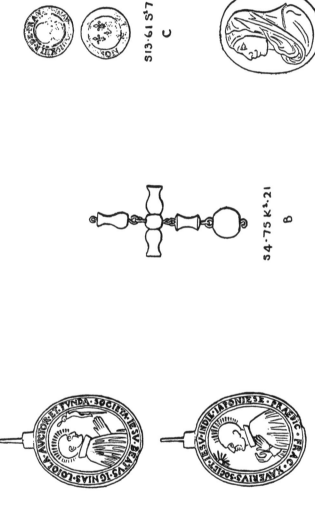

Fig. 23. Medallions, coin, and rosary fragment. Length of A, 1 3/16 inches; of B, 2 1/2 inches; of C, 11/16 inches; of D, 13/16 inches.

weighed 3.6 gm., and the second 2 inches long and weighed 6 gm.

Plate (Pl. xxv). Approximately one-half of a complete plate or shallow bowl was found near the southeast corner of the central fireplace under a mass of burnt clay and other débris. The original vessel had had a flat rim 1 inch wide, rolled under along the edge. The diameter of the vessel was about 7 inches. Whether it was for secular or religious use is unknown, probably the latter (Pl. xxv *a*).

Spigot. A brass spigot found on the site has already been described on page 121.

Coin (Fig. 23). A very badly corroded copper coin was identified by Mr. Classey of the Museum and expedition staff as a double tournois of Louis XIII (1610-43). Its diameter was ¾ of an inch. The place of finding was the 13th level of 61S[1] (the storage pit) (Fig. 23, C).

Instrument (Pl. L). A delicate instrument very much like a modern square in outline lay in the very corner of the northeast bastion. The flat arms were ¼ inch wide; one was 2½ and the other 1⅝ inches long. At each end was a hook or curl, the direction of which was the same in both. No marks of any kind were discernible, for it was slightly corroded (Pl. L, D).

Copper-sheathed Object. A specimen whose use cannot be surmised was made of bone, with the flat surfaces covered by very thin sheets of copper held in place with six small rivets. Its general outline was reel-shaped, or rectangular with the long sides concave. It was 2 inches by 1⅛ inches. It lay in the second level of 81C[2], that is, some distance east of the east curtain and south of the northeast bastion.

Grill. A section of what appears to have been a copper grill was found in two parts in 83W. Slender strips of metal were riveted together to form an openwork pattern.

Wire. Two and possibly three pieces of copper wire were recovered from areas evidently undisturbed.

Kettle Fragments. Included in the collection are a good many strips of brass which showed trough-like depressions similar to those on certain kettles, which suggests that they were scraps cut from such articles. Indeed, one is inclined to think that much of the sheet brass on the site was so derived.

From the same or similar sources may have come the numerous little objects apparently cut to shape, such as oblongs, rectangles, and squares. Many were perforated as if for attachment to some object, while others actually retained 1½ inch nails used in conjunction with them.

Composites. Certain specimens illustrated the combined use of brass and iron in one object presumably necessitated by the scarcity of metal. One good example consisted of an iron strap to which was riveted a similar strap of brass. In some cases, instead of rivets, little snips of brass were used to hold the composite article together.

Riveted Pieces. A large number of brass objects were riveted together in twos or threes. They must have been more or less in the nature of patches or improvisations.

Nuggets. In several instances nuggets of metal were found, the largest of which is illustrated in Pl. L, B.

Unidentified Objects. Numerous objects cannot be identified, farther than to say that they seem to have been made for a definite purpose. A good example is seen at (A) in Plate L, where a well-made, perforated plate is shown. Other specimens, somewhat resembling modern gaskets, are shown on the same plate at (C) and (M).

Lead (Pl. XLVIII). A few samples of lead bore testimony to its use by the founders of Ste Marie. All told, these numbered only about eighteen, of which seven were pieces of shot (see p. 125). One object of lead resembled the head of a rivet, which had been cut off; another was a very thick-walled tube 1 9/16 inches long. The rest were irregular, rough strips.

A small triangular piece from the rim of a little vessel, probably a mug, may be described here, although it was of some other metal than lead. It was hard and white, and exact identification of material has not been made.

All lead objects were found in the vicinity of the workshop.

Silver (Fig. 20, 23). Few silver objects were discovered on the site. Most notable of those found were the medallion (its composition is not absolutely certain), and the silver needle-case described on page 118. A description of the medallion is given on page 144.

A third specimen, apparently silver, consisted of an oval plate, exceedingly thin, upon which was stamped the impression of a man's bust, facing left, draped in a cloth headgear which hung loosely over the shoulder in front. The face was strong, with full lips and chin, large eye, and receding forehead. The hair was concealed under the headgear. Apparently the piece was mounted for a ring or locket, for part of the rim or bezel was attached to it when it was discovered. Its length was 13/16 inches and its width 10/16 inches. The portrait appeared to be that of a layman (Fig. 23, D).

V. MODERN SPECIMENS

Apparently modern were a copper bell, very like a sleigh bell, a copper medal, and a brass buckle. The medal may be worth describing here, since it was obviously dropped on the site by a traveller or a pilgrim. It was oval, not unlike the one described below (p. 144), and bore on one face an impression of Ste Winnifred of Wales, and on the other the words "Souvenir of Holywell." The medal lay near the surface along the false wall. The brass buckle came from a nineteenth-century costume.

(b) Crockery and Pottery

It was not always possible to distinguish between pottery of ancient European manufacture and modern wares found on the site. Many pieces were discarded as very modern and of no archaeological interest; the remainder has been divided into two groups according to apparent age.

Modern. The presumably modern group includes seven pieces of white clay tobacco pipes, such as were popular fifty years ago in this country; a brown glaze earthenware ink pot and thirty-six fragments of a green glaze crockery. Most of this latter material lay on or near the surface; this circumstance, taken in conjunction with the fact that the green was bluish as against a yellowish green on ancient material, leads one to identify it as modern.

A piece of ornate white clay pipe stem from the fifth level of 87Q¹ was 1¼ inches long with a clean break at each end where there was a raised ring. It was pressed in a mould bearing an

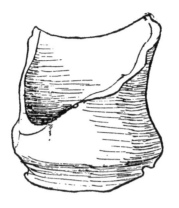

$$S4 \cdot 56 \, A^2 \cdot 2$$

A

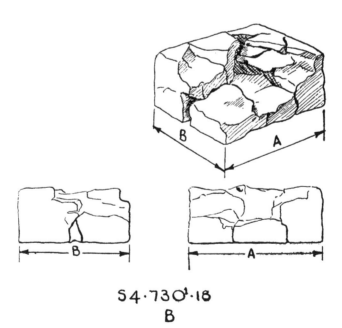

$$S4 \cdot 730^2 \cdot 18$$

B

Fig. 24. European clay vessel and brick. Scale: A, 1:1; B, 1:3.

intricate design of flowers and leaves. It was probably of nine-teenth-century make.

Seventeenth-Century Pottery (Fig. 24). Twenty-seven sherds may be classified as sevententh-century European ware. Some of it was extremely crude. One large fragment, for instance, was made of a friable red paste, unglazed, and appeared to be part of a ring base from a large pot; and another which was melted in the conflagration seemed to have been part of a pipe stem. Of a much harder paste and wheel-turned, but still unglazed, were five fragments. One piece of this material was the bottom part of a small jar, the sides of which were concave. It lay in the south-east bastion, and still contained what appeared to be ash. The diameter was 1⅝ inches (Fig. 24, A). A large rim sherd found in 730[1] near the central fireplace was exceptional in that the paste was exceedingly hard and a dark grey. To judge from the frag-ment, the vessel was globular and much constricted at the neck. The rim of the neck was ½ inch deep and everted, with an orifice 3½ inches in diameter.

Nineteen sherds showed a glaze, usually brown or green. Two, however, one from the base of a jar or bowl, and the other from a flat handle, showed a poor type of reddish-brown glaze. The paste in all was soft. The green lead glazes varied from light yellowish green to a deeper tone of the same hue, often showing a slightly mottled effect; and the tone was frequently deeper on the interior surface. It had chipped off in numerous places. One rim sherd indicated by its shape that it had come from a small crock. As judged by its curvature, the largest sherd came from the wall of a jar not exceeding 2½ inches in diameter. The green-glazed crockery was found chiefly in 67Q[1] with stray sherds in 64L[1] and 83Y[1].

An extremely deep green glaze was present on the exterior of eight small sherds. Three appeared to be the bottoms of tiny jars with flat bases and expanding sides.

One or two other sherds had glazes which may have been due to accidental circumstances. It was demonstrable from bits of Indian pottery in the collection that when it was subjected to a temperature sufficiently high, the paste fused, became porous, very light in weight compared to its size, and the exterior solidified to a deep brown glaze.

(c) Glass

Exclusive of glass beads, a number of specimens of glass were recovered from the site. Modern material, which comprised more than half of the collection, has no special interest for us here, and will not be referred to further. The fifty-four samples which are known or thought to be of seventeenth-century origin or older were found under the following conditions:

(1) Twenty-six were discovered in locations showing no evidence of disturbance, except that in six of these cases the glass itself had certain modern attributes.

(2) Twenty-one pieces came from areas known from other evidence to have been disturbed but which by analogy with material in (1) are acceptable as seventeenth-century glass.

(3) Seven specimens were found in the first level but bore some evidence of antiquity in shape, metal, or colour.

The areas of greatest concentration were near the south end, particularly the southwest corner of the Residence, in the storage pit, and near the well. Also, small fragments were scattered without discernible pattern over most of the site.

When age was in doubt, it has been assessed by weighing evidence of several types. The knowledge and experience of Mr. F. St. G. Spendlove, of the Royal Ontario Museum staff, have been extensively drawn upon and generously given. Direct comparison with museum specimens of documented origin and with site specimens of class (1) above has been made.

The condition of the specimen, that is, the degree of preservation or disintegration of the metal itself, has not been taken into consideration in estimating age because a comparison of a small number of specimens readily shows how untrustworthy is such a gauge. Two fragments from the same vessel, lying not far apart, may show great variation in the degree to which they have decomposed, depending apparently on slight differences in soil condition, heat, drainage, and the like.

For descriptive purposes, the samples of glass from Ste Marie have been classified into: I. material known to be of seventeenth-century origin because discovered in undisturbed locations; II. material believed on internal evidence to be from the seventeenth century; III. material of indeterminate origin.

I. MATERIAL KNOWN TO BE OF SEVENTEENTH-CENTURY ORIGIN

The group includes three more or less complete specimens and a small number of fragments.

Spectacle lens. Found in the 3rd level of 87Q[1], at the edge of the well. Because it had been broken across the centre, it had been discarded. Oval and slightly concavo-convex, it had diameters of 27.5 and 23.5 mm. A dense, chalky patina obscured the nature of the metal, which seemed now to be highly crystalline.

Drop-shaped bottle. Lying on the vegetable refuse, or rather embedded in it, in a totally undisturbed condition in the storage pit, were the remains of a large drop-shaped bottle. Most of the fragments were small; the largest was the tubular neck, which was but slightly damaged. It may be seen *in situ* in Plate x *a*. As the pieces came out they were covered with a rich, golden patina which on drying tended to flake or rub off. When this happened, the surface was left striated, showing how the metal had been drawn out in blowing and cooling. All fragments were carefully collected and later pieced together by Mr. William Todd, museum preparator, in the hope that at least the general outlines and dimensions could be determined. It was an exceedingly delicate task, both on account of the multitude of small bits into which the vessel had been broken, and on account of their extreme thinness. Moreover, the fractured surfaces had eroded somewhat, making it difficult to get adhesives to hold and diminishing the area of the surface of the vessel as a whole. In the end, however, the vessel was restored, as may be seen in the frontispiece. A few fragments could not be fitted in, others were entirely lacking; so that two large holes, not visible in the plate, still exist, as well as a number of small ones. In spite of these deficiencies, the vessel as it stands is a splendid achievement in restoration.

The vessel may be described as drop-shaped. The slender, tubular neck expands rather suddenly into the oval body, which has a concave bottom. Like all blown glass, it is somewhat asymmetrical. The graceful lines and pleasing proportions mark it as a splendid example of the blower's art. The metal appeared to be a very pale green, not entirely without bubbles. The walls are extremely thin, averaging about ½ mm. in thickness, or even less.

The metal, colour, and shape of this exquisite vessel indicate a Venetian origin and together with the extreme thinness of the glass point to the end of the sixteenth century as a likely date.

We may speculate on its having been given to the Jesuit Fathers as a parting gift from some noble or wealthy patron of their missionary work. And the story of its dangerous journey across the ocean, up the St. Lawrence and Ottawa Rivers and across country by way of the Mattawa and French Rivers to its final resting place at Fort Ste Marie, would make a saga in itself. We shall probably never know where it was shattered (but not irreparably!) into fragments; it could have happened on the journey and not been discovered until it was unpacked, or it may have done long and honourable duty at Ste Marie until, broken at last, it was thrown away. Restored now to something like its original condition, it stands out as one of the fine examples of early European glass in the New World, and was probably the first of all real art treasures to reach Canadian shores.

The following are approximate measurements:

Height: 246 mm. (not including rim) (circ. 9¾ ins.)

Maximum diameter: 122 mm. (circ. 5 ins.)

Neck: Maximum diameter: 22 mm. (circ. 1 in.)

Minimum diameter: 18 mm. (circ. ⅝ ins.)

Length: 85 mm. (circ. 3¼ ins.)

(*Drop-shaped?*) *Bottle.* The fragmentary remains of a vessel which appeared to be very similar to that described above were found near it in the storage pit. The shape and size of the two vessels, judging principally from the neck, were about the same; the metal was probably a paler green in the present specimen and slightly thicker. Decomposition had advanced much further in this glass and what remained of it was highly crystalline and brittle. The fragments remaining were heavily patinated to a deep, rich gold, except the inner surface of the neck, which was smooth and clean. The surface under the patina showed the same striation as seen in the previous specimen.

No restoration has been possible here, although probably as much as one-quarter of the original vessel was recovered. For comparison, approximate measurements are given:

Length of neck: 85 mm.

Diameter of neck: 22 mm.

Maximum thickness of neck: 2 mm.

Minimum thickness of neck: 1 mm.

Fragments. Five fragments (Cat. S6-67Q¹-1), apparently all from the same vessel, were of a pale green metal, about ½ mm. thick, with a "watered" surface inside and out. This surface texture may have been original, or it may have been brought about secondarily by painting or some other treatment. The fragments appeared to be from a bottle.

A fragment of pale green glass (Cat. S8-65N¹-8) was probably from the wall of a moderate-sized vessel. It had many of the earmarks of Venetian glass. There was no patination.

Five specimens of a heavy white glass which had decomposed extensively, patinated to a deep black, come from squares 63L¹, 65L¹, 66Y¹, 69M¹, and 71Q¹. Nearly all were so crystalline as to crumble along the edges when touched, where they often showed a golden hue owing to the patination of the crystals. Thickness varied from 1 to 5 mm.; curvatures suggest that the pieces came from the corners of squarish vessels or bottles. This variety was the most massive of the old glass.

Six small fragments of green glass with plane surfaces were relatively but not uniformly thin and patinated to a light gold in varying degrees.

II. MATERIAL ASSIGNED ON INTERNAL EVIDENCE TO THE SEVENTEENTH
   CENTURY

Into this group have been put those specimens which, on comparison with glass known to date from the seventeenth century, showed more similarities thereto than to products of a later date. Most of the specimens were found in disturbed soil.

Ten examples of the heavy white glass with deep black patination like that described above were found in disturbed levels. On account of their similarity to the undisturbed material it seems reasonable to ascribe them to the seventeenth century.

Three specimens of the pale-green, plane-surfaced glass described above were likewise discovered in disturbed soil, but because of their similarity to undoubted seventeenth-century material are listed here.

The rim of a small bottle was found in a much-disturbed area beside the moat in the first exploratory trench to be opened. It was a pale green glass which appeared rather darker than the other green glass because of its greater thickness. It was relatively free of bubbles. The marked asymmetry indicated definitely that it was blown. The rim was decidedly flaring. (Diameter: 27 mm.; maximum thickness: 2 mm.).

A piece of glass, unusually white for seventeenth-century material, was found in an apparently unlisturbed level in 75K[1]. An extremely thin fragment from the wall of a bottle was found in the lowest disturbed level in 65L[1]. It was an unusually pale green, patinated to a pale metallic gold.

III. MATERIAL OF INDETERMINATE ORIGIN

Into this group have been brought all those samples of glass about which there was insufficient evidence to warrant assigning them to any of the above categories. In three cases the specimens came from squares showing no other evidence of disturbance. The remainder came either from disturbed levels or were found so crose to the surface as to throw their origin into doubt.

Compared with the glass described above, these specimens were thick and heavy, like the glass in old-fashioned medicine bottles and flasks. Most of it was relatively white; at least three pieces, however, were greenish. All showed some degree of patination, varying from the merest film to one heavy enough to flake off and leave a roughened surface. The patination was usually of a metallic creamy hue, strongly shot with purple. Some pieces may have derived from a seventeenth-century European glassworks.

The following examples from this class may have some interest:

Cat. S4-61K[1]-5. From the corner of a bottle. Pale green in metal, it had a purplish patina. The thickness was 2.5 mm.

Cat. S8-62H[1]-2. A pale green glass, 5 mm. thick, from a large bottle. Very faintly patinated purplish.

Cat. S1-66Z-1. From the slightly concave bottom of a large bottle or flask. Very pale green, patinated creamy, and about 3 mm. to 5 mm. thick.

Cat. S1-65B[1]-1. From the cylindrical neck of a flask. Pale green, patinated creamy. About 3 mm. thick.

Cat. S1-85H[1]-2. A heavy piece of pale green bottle glass, slightly patinated metallic purple and gold. From the walls of a large bottle. From 3.5 mm. to 8 mm. thick.

(d) Bone

About ten thousand fragments of bone were scattered over the site, with especially large concentrations in the area of the Residence, particularly in the fill north of the foundation wall, on and near the hearths, east of the northwest bastion, and in the Indian hearths. Exclusive of a few hundred specimens of modern origin, such as beef bones, and the skeletons of small animals, chiefly rodents, most of the material bore evidence of having been refuse from meals. Much of it had been boiled; some of it was partially burned, especially that found on the hearth. By far the greater number of specimens consisted of small fragments of large bones and the bones of small birds, fish, and mammals. There were also a good many large bones, particularly the leg bones of birds and a few mammal bones.

From what has already been said, it is apparent that mammals, birds, and fish were used for food, with mammals and birds seemingly predominant. Fish bones were not, however, uncommon. The identification of species is being carried out by the Royal Ontario Museum of Zoology. It is hoped to publish a brief separate report on the bones when the work of identification is complete. It is probable that while the majority of the bones are of wild, indigenous species, domesticated animals may also be represented.

Bones found in Indian hearths and closely associated with Indian artifacts, as well as bones which were obviously deposited after the burning of the site, for example, those found on the threshold of the southwest bastion door, were refuse discarded by the Hurons. It is presumed that most of the remainder had been used by the French occupants of the site.

Few artifacts of bone came to light. Of European origin were the rosary beads and the peculiar copper-sheathed bone object described on page 130.

(e) Beads

A moderate-sized collection of beads—some ninety-three counting both complete and fragmentary specimens—comprised a wide variety of types. The bone beads, of which there were eleven specimens, exclusive of five still in position in a fragmentary rosary, were presumably for ritual purposes; the remainder, of

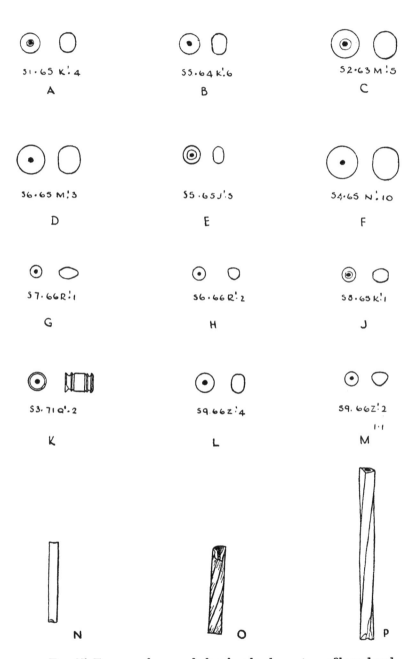

FIG. 25. European bone and glass beads, shown in profile and end views. Scale: about 2:3.

glass, were so like the usual trade bead that we may safely assume that they were imported for the same purpose.

Bone beads (Fig. 25). The bone beads were frequently very well preserved and still retained a high lustre (Fig. 25, C-F). Several were of a deep black, though most were a rich, natural straw-colour, and a few were grayish from lying in ash or from calcination. Ten of them were globular, with the ends slightly flattened, and measured from ¼ to ½ inch in diameter. A unique, barrel-shaped bead is shown in Fig. 25K.

Glass Beads. Of sixty-five glass beads, forty-five were red and the rest blue. The blue beads were mostly globular, though two were oblong, almost elliptical, and one was tubular. Two shades of blue, a light and a dark, were used in making these beads, with the dark much preferred. All blue beads, unlike red ones, have weathered, to some extent. A beautiful blue bead, 1 5/16 inches long, had six spiral grooves. The usual dimensions for the round beads were 3/16 to 5/16 inches in diameter and 3/16 to ¼ inches in length.

The red beads were either round or tubular and the latter might be round or square in section. The two classes were nearly equal numerically. In measurement, the round beads ranged from ⅛ to ¼ inches. Apparently none of the tubular beads was complete, for their ends nearly always looked unfinished. Those which were round in section were much the more numerous, the ratio being about 3 to 1. Lengths varied from ⅛ to ¼ inches and diameters from ⅛ to ¼ inches. Of the five tubular beads with square sections, three were twisted spirally, though not one of the round-sectioned specimens was so formed. Lengths varied from ⅜ to 2⅜ inches.

The round red beads varied in colour. Usually they were a solid, rather dull, coral red throughout, but slightly less than half of them had a core of colourless glass. Casual inspection left one with the impression that the core was black, but a closer scrutiny showed that this was due to the masking effect of the outer layer of red (Fig. 25, A, B, G-J, L, M).

(f) Articles of Religious Use

There can be little doubt that when the surviving missionaries finally left Ste Marie I, they took with them those articles of

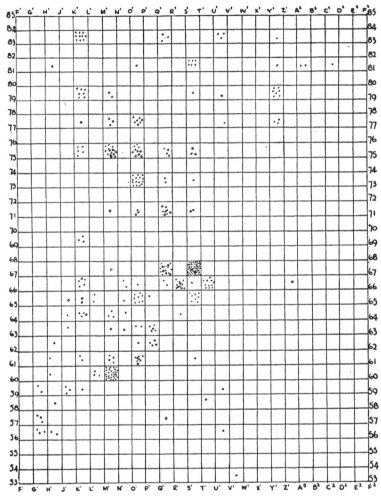

DISTRIBUTION PLAN 1. Distribution of beads and Indian sherds in the compound area.

chapel use and religious significance which they still possessed. The few specimens of this kind remaining must only have been such as had been lost on the site during the course of its habitation, or had been discarded or overlooked in the final departure.

Medallion (Fig. 23, A). Most significant of these was a silver or bronze medallion about an inch long and oval in outline, found near the surface in the 66-Trench, west of the compound. It was unusually well preserved, except for a slight chip on the rim near the bottom, and a heavy black patina. Between medallion and eye was a small flange to which the oval eye itself was so fixed that its plane was at right angles to the plane of the object. The obverse bore a figure, facing right, in the position of adoration before a small crucifix, and the inscription:

BEATUS. IGNIAS. LOIOLA. AUCTOR. ET. FUNDA. SOCIETA. IESU. *

The figure, with shaven head surrounded by a sort of halo, wore a flowing robe with a high collar. The reverse bore a figure similarly attired but with hands crossed high on the chest, and facing the left towards a radiate orb. The inscription encircling the figure read:

FRAC. XAVERIUS. SOCIETA. IESU. INDIE. IAPONESE. PRAEDIC. *

In connection with these it will be noted that the reference was rather to the "Blessed Ignatius Loyola" than to "Saint Ignatius Loyola," an indication that the medallion was struck previous to his canonization which occurred in 1622.

Iron Bells (Pl. xlviii). Two small iron bells were of a type long used in the celebration of the Mass. They were semi-globular, with the clapper attachment at the apex of the inside. One of them was provided with a tripartite attachment, indicating that the specimen had originally three clappers, although only one remained. Such altar bells are said still to be in use in certain places. The other bell was similar to the one just described, but smaller, less well preserved, and had no clapper when found. Both lay in the southwest corner of the compound, one of them inside the southwest bastion (Pl. xlviii, A, H).

Copper Plate (Pl. xxv *a*). The copper plate of which a fragment was found near the central hearth (pp. 51, 130), may possibly

*The following free translation of these inscriptions has kindly been supplied by Father Lally: "Blessed Ignatius Loyola, Founder and General of the Society of Jesus"; and, "Francis Xavier, of the Society of Jesus, missionary to India and Japan."

have been reserved for sacred use, and so may a variety of other specimens, including the fine glass.

Rosaries (Fig. 23). As already mentioned, a large section from a rosary lay on the wooden floor west of the central hearth in the Residence. It was strung on fine silver wire, which, unfortunately, had become so brittle as to require repairing in several places. The specimen consisted of four bone beads, all differently shaped, and arranged in a cruciform pattern. The top bead was vasiform. The one below it was so carved that each side was shaped like a small vasiform bead while the centre was globular. The third from the top was spool-shaped and the bottom one globular (Fig. 23, B).

Since this fragment was undoubtedly part of a rosary and since bone beads very similar to those on the fragment were found elsewhere, it is presumed that these too were originally parts of rosaries.

SPECIMENS OF INDIAN ORIGIN

(a) Pottery

Tobacco Pipes (Fig. 26, 27). A modest collection of Indian clay pipe fragments was recovered from the site, fifty-eight pieces in all. Eleven lay outside the compound, sixteen between the south end of the Residence and the southwest bastion, three in the Residence, and a small number were scattered over the rest of the compound, almost always in association with other Indian and European material. There is no doubt, however, that the specimens were of native manufacture, showing no influence from contact in material, form, decoration or in any other respect.

Not a single pipe was complete. Nevertheless, there were six complete bowls and seven complete stems. The latter were from 2⅞ to 3½ inches long, so that the originals were probably about 4 or 4½ inches in length. They all seem to have belonged to the "elbow" type, with a greater or lesser angle at the bend. Of the thirty-seven stem fragments, thirty were plain; the others had simple designs which we may take as fairly representative of Huron work. The simplest consisted of a raised crest or ridge running lengthwise of the upper side of the stem; an elaboration of

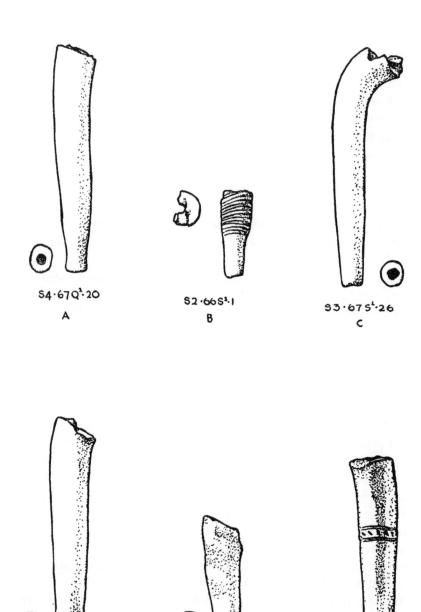

S4·67Q².20
A

S2·66S².1
B

S3·67S⁴·26
C

55·62P³·5
D

S4·66X·1
E

S2·71Q⁴·5
F

Fɪɢ. 26. Clay pipe stems of Huron Indian manufacture. Scale:
about 2:3.

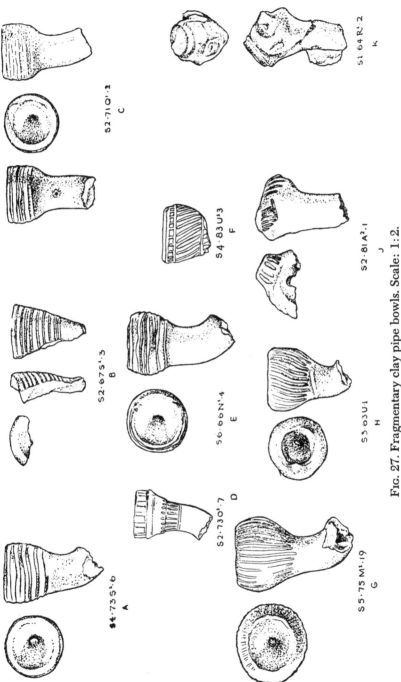

Fɪɢ. 27. Fragmentary clay pipe bowls. Scale: 1:2.

this, seen on another fragment, consisted of a row of punctate marks along each side of the crest. Another applied design was that in which shallow circular grooves were drawn around the stem; in one such design two grooves enclosed a band of punctate marks (Fig. 26, F). Modelled designs, rarer than applied, were shown on one stem which had a serpentine twist (Fig. 26, E), and in another which had a ring about ¼ inch from the near end. The basic form of pipe stems was that of a slender cone.

The basic forms of pipe bowls were three in number: (*a*) zoomorphic, (*b*) globular, and (*c*) geometric. The first was represented in the collection by a fragment of a bowl in the shape of a stylized bird (Fig. 27, J), and in another fragment showing a human head about 1⅛ inches in diameter, modelled in the round and supported on the rim (Fig. 27, K). Such pipes usually had the head facing the smoker. The figure portrayed was wearing a flat circular cap; the features were stylized to a considerable extent.

The simple globular form was well shown in a large specimen found in the Residence, the exterior of which was finely marked with numerous, shallow vertical grooves beginning at the base of the bowl and ending at the edge of the convex rim (Fig. 27, G). Another specimen was similarly marked, except that the grooves curved slightly to the right towards the rim (Fig. 27, H). In a further modification, the curve was to the left and there were two horizontal grooves just below the rim. In the extreme form, the bowl had become almost bell-shaped with a fluted, vertical rim and the grooves had been reduced to arrow-like markings (Fig. 27, D). This bowl was the most elaborate discovered on the site; its high polish, black lustre, and fine workmanship indicated that it was a carefully made specimen. Globular pipes with horizontal grooves are well known in the Huron country; the collection contained nine examples. Bowls with six grooves were most numerous, with those of seven following; there was one each with two, four, five, and nine grooves. The workmanship varied from crude to very good; the grooves had been made with some blunt object, usually they were rather shallow and on all but one bowl had been smoothed off subsequently to remove the rough edges. A very simple form of the globular type was trumpet-shaped with a thick rim (Fig. 27, A, C, E).

The geometric form, apparently very uncommon, was here represented by one small fragment; it had a thick wall with a circular interior but a perpendicular flat-faced exterior, probably six- or eight-sided.

Huron pipes were generally better made than other Huron pottery whether because of more careful selection of clays, or better firing, or both. The biscuit appeared much harder as a rule and finer grained; coarse tempering was rare. The natural colour was a yellowish to whitish buff, with darker blotches due to uneven firing. In twenty-five instances in the collection, precautions were taken to blacken the material, doubtless by rubbing the surface with grease and then burning the grease away so that the soot was left in the pores, or by holding it in dense smoke; the results were frequently uneven. Both naturally coloured and blackened pipes were often given a high polish; nearly half of all specimens were so treated.

Sherds of Vessels (Fig. 28, 29). Practically all parts of the site wherever excavation was done yielded sherds of Indian pottery—294 pieces in all. They were particularly abundant in the south end of the compound, especially near the central ditch, and in the Residence and along the west wall of the Chapel. This prevalence is understandable when we recall that the Indians must have used the place extensively, even into Jesuit times, and that the Jesuits themselves probably bought and used native pots for many purposes (see Distribution Plan, p. 143).

No entire, or even nearly entire, vessels were discovered. In a few cases, several sherds could be pieced together to make larger fragments; one reconstructed piece was made from eight small sherds, and this largest specimen only comprised about 1/5 or 1/6 of the original. Nevertheless, there were many cases where sherds came obviously from the same vessel, but since the intervening sections were missing the whole could not be reconstructed. It was not always true that sherds found together belonged to the same vessel; sometimes they did, but not infrequently matching sherds were found considerable distances apart, and contiguous sherds were of diverse shapes. In view of this, it is impossible to say how many pots were represented in the collection, but there seemed to be a fairly large number, judging by variations in decoration and design.

All the Indian sherds seemed to be Huron, although some of them were found in situations which indicate a later period than the Jesuit occupation. For instance, numerous sherds, including many which could be pieced together, were found in the central ditch, not far from the surface, above the charred boards which had been placed there. If not actually Huron, they were at least definitely Iroquoian, and made by the methods described by Wintemberg. The paste was a hard, buff clay, tempered in varying degrees with crushed quartz. In thinner-walled vessels the firing was satisfactory; in vessels with thicker walls, it is usual to see a grey or black core which had been insufficiently heated.

There was no slip, and no evidence of painting, nor even of burnishing, on the pots. Differences in colours were due to firing or to subsequent staining in use.

So far as the fragmentary condition of the pottery will permit us to judge, the vessels were not large. The largest appears to have had a diameter of about 8 inches. The common form was globular, and castellations were favoured; they were found on six sherds. Two sherds indicated the use of a vessel of general globular form, but so depressed that there was a pronounced, almost angular, shoulder. All rim sherds except one showed a constriction below the rim, but it was never very pronounced. Usually the rim itself was thickened sufficiently to make its exterior form vertical, but this was not always the case. The depth of the rim was usually ½ to 1 inch. The thickest sherd of Indian origin was about 1½ inches through, which was about twice the thickness of most. Typical cross-sections are illustrated in Figs. 28 and 29.

Decoration, confined in every case to the exterior of vessels, was generally sparingly applied and consisted of incised lines or grooves, rows of small punctate marks drawn either with the finger-nail or a blunt object, little nubbins left by way of decoration (one example), the castellations already mentioned, and a haphazard stippling of the surface with little depressions (two examples). The grooving took the form of hatching on thirty-eight sherds. Fifteen of them were simple bands of hatching on rims, either dextral or sinistral; the sixteenth was cross-hatching on a rim sherd. Frequently one length of a rim was hatched sinis-

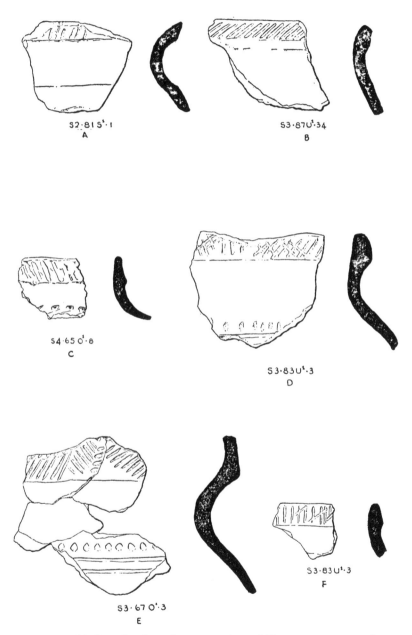

S2·8I5¹·I
A

S3·87U¹·34
B

S4·65 0¹·8
C

S3·83U¹·3
D

S3·67 0¹·3
E

S3·83U¹·3
F

Fɪɢ. 28. Rim sherds and cross-sections of Huron pottery vessels.
Scale: 1:2.

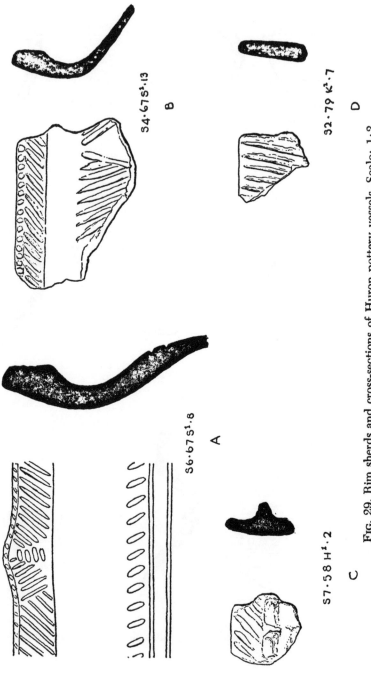

36·67 s¹·8

A

34·67 s¹·13

B

57·58 H¹·2

C

32·79 K²·7

D

Fig. 29. Rim sherds and cross-sections of Huron pottery vessels. Scale: 1:3.

trally, and a corresponding length dextrally, with a castellation separating them. A number of sherds showed that hatching was often done so that an area—usually a triangle—was hatched at right angles to adjacent areas, but this condition was not present in any rim sherds in the collection, so we may assume that it was a shoulder design. The shoulders of two rim sherds were hatched in one direction only. Below the rim there was usually an undecorated band—the constriction; below this, on the shoulder, there might be the hatching already described, or one or more horizontal grooves, or one or more rows of punctate depressions. Grooves and depressions sometimes appeared on the same shoulder, but hatching does not seem to have been used on shoulders in conjunction with either of the other elements, though they might all occur on the same vessel. The horizontal grooves appeared only in one instance on a rim sherd, where four of them constituted the only decoration (Fig. 29).

In summary, it may be said that, as exemplified by material from Ste Marie, Huron pottery was grit-tempered, moderately well fired, and consisted principally of globular and depressed globular forms frequently castellated and decorated by bands of incised hatching, horizontal grooves, and punctate marks. Rarely was it characterized by all-over stippling with a sharp instrument or by a row of projecting nubbins. Two sherds show "pie-crust" rims.

Included in the collection were seventy-two pieces of pottery which were made apparently of local clay, and according to native methods for the most part, but which in some cases were too dense, and in all cases were too thick and incorrectly shaped to be of Indian origin. One good-sized specimen was a handle from a large vessel about an inch thick. Others appeared to be rim and side-walls from very thick, cylindrical jars, some of which bore horizontal or vertical decorative grooves. The decoration was always extremely simple, even rudimentary. Approximately thirty of these specimens were fragments from the sides of a cylinder, or cylinders, an inch thick, faceted on the exterior so that in section the object was octagonal with a round bore. The diameter of the original cylinder was about 3 inches. The longest section recovered was 4 inches. Their function is entirely unknown, unless they may have been moulds.

It was possible by piecing together numerous fragments found along the eastward-projecting wall of the central fireplace to make a partial restoration of a large clay vessel resembling a modern bulb-bowl, but deeper. The bottom was flat, the sides slightly convex, and the rim somewhat thickened (Pl. xxvii *a*).

A possible explanation of this crude material is that it was made by Indians under French tutelage. We know that it was the aim of the Jesuits to introduce European crafts among the Hurons, and in teaching pottery, new shapes and new techniques would be introduced. The presence of these fragments could therefore be attributed to the first efforts of Hurons to make pots in European styles, while largely retaining native techniques.

(b) *Bone and Antler*

Fragments of an antler ladle lay close to the outside of the south wall of the central hearth at floor level. They were slightly calcined, but not enough to destroy their identity. Not all the pieces could be found, but enough were recovered to permit of some of them being fitted together to show the general outline of the object from which they had come. It was evidently a small spoon or ladle, with a shallow bowl, about 9 inches long. The transition between handle and bowl was gradual, and at the head of the handle the material was carved to the shape of a duck's head. Indeed, the outline of the object leaves no doubt that the maker intended it to have the appearance of a duck in flight, with outstretched neck. It was remarkably well done; only the lines necessary to convey the impression were used, yet the subject was clear and unmistakable. The bowl, now incomplete, was oval in outline (Fig. 30, B).

The tip end of a bone harpoon point or dart point was found. It was about 3 inches long, ½ inch wide, and rather roughly shaped with three barbs along one side and none on the other.

No other artifacts of bone could be identified among the material from the site.

(c) *Stone*

The stone material gleaned from the site was interesting, if not extensive. Besides chert scrapers and numerous cores and

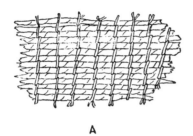

A

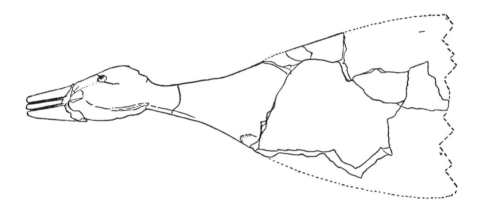

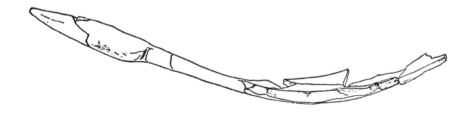

S5·830³·4

B

Fig. 30. Huron textile fabric and antler ladle. Scale: about 1:3.

flakes, there were a few heavier tools, including a stone axe, a tobacco pipe of limestone, several lumps of mineral pigments, and a piece of mica. There was no slate, however, nor were there any arrow or spear-points. The stone objects found might be classified as domestic tools, and objects of ritual use. They threw an interesting light upon a hitherto almost unknown phase of Huron activity, and are the more valuable since they were for the most part datable.

Scrapers and Drills (Fig. 31). The total number of chert specimens was ninety-six, of which seventy-three were small flakes, two cores and one drill, and the remainder scrapers. The material was generally a grey chert of variable quality, similar to that from beds on the Huron shore. It was much inferior to that from Flint Ridge, Ohio, and large nuggets of it were probably always rare. Two cores and one scraper were yellow in colour, almost like jasper. No European flint came to light.

If the distribution of chert is plotted, most of it will be seen to have occurred in the workshop area, and the south end of the compound generally, with very little elsewhere.

The scrapers conformed to a single type, shown in the illustration (Fig. 31, B, C), namely turtle-backs. They were usually short rectangles, showing secondary chipping along three sides with the fourth side left unfinished. The side opposite that left unfinished was steeply bevelled. Sometimes the shorter, and sometimes the longer side of the rectangle was prepared for actual use. The workmanship was tolerably good but cannot be described as fine.

An extraordinary chert object found in 62P^1, probably used as a scraper, was almost axe-shaped, being rectangular with a convex bit and a rather heavy poll. It was heavily calcined, owing no doubt to exposure to the fire. Its dimensions were 1¼ inches by ⅞ inch, whereas other scrapers from the site were 1 inch by 13/16 inch on the average.

Most scrapers found elsewhere in the Huron and Petun country which the writer has seen were longer than those from Ste Marie, being of the type frequently called thumb-nail scrapers. The drill had a quadrilateral head and a short shaft (Fig. 31, A).

Axe (Pl. xxviii). An oval granite stone, broken at one end,

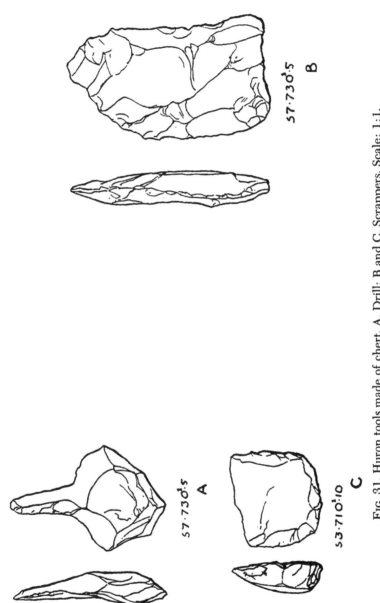

FIG. 31. Huron tools made of chert. A, Drill; B and C, Scrappers. Scale: 1:1.

was found in 63D[1]. Its shape and smooth surface indicate that it was used as a grinding stone. A smaller granite pebble, nearly round except for one side and one end which had been chiselled flat, was possibly a grinder also; it was found in the southwest bastion. A large and well-made axe of fine granite lay near the top of the stone wall which formed the back of the Chapel fireplace. The tool was about 9 inches long, all sides and surfaces convex, so that a cross-section taken at any point along its length would be elliptical. Its location when found and its generally finished appearance suggest that it was of Algonkian rather than of Huron manufacture. The lithic industry of the Hurons, while very imperfectly known, is thought to have been incapable of producing a tool so well made (Pl. xxviii *a*).

A lump of rock containing a quantity of mica lay in 54G[1].

Pigments. Seven pieces of mineral pigment looked somewhat like lumps of limestone, except that they contained pockets of a powdery yellow substance, resembling yellow ochre. A large lump of porous rock showed patches of a vermilion substance which rubbed off readily but clung tenaciously to the skin. Fifteen specimens yielded a red pigment; two of these were heavy stone in which the pigment lay and rubbed off easily. Most of the others were hard nodules, probably of hematite, which had to be rubbed forcibly before the colour would come off. Very likely, pigments of this sort were ground and mixed with grease when applied. In two instances an ochreous red was produced by a soft, powdery mineral, not unlike limestone except in colour. A bright red sandstone in the collection may have been prized for its colour. Except for the last mentioned, the pigments have not been identified, but the red substances were probably hematite and the yellow substances were caused by iron salts in some such vehicle as limestone.

Pipe (Pl. xxix). The bowl of a tobacco pipe fashioned of limestone was found in the fourth level of 66S[1]. It was made to simulate a bird, the body constituting the bowl. Features were not indicated, but the head was simply carved, and at the rear of the bowl the wing feathers folded gracefully to form the tail (Pl. xxix *c*).

(d) Textile

In squares 71H¹ to 71K¹, buried in undisturbed soil, lay a piece of textile. Part of it rested directly on charred wood from the Residence, presumably wall boards (Pl. xxviii c). Like the wood, the textile was extensively charred, and to this it owed its preservation. At least in some places it was doubled—a fact which greatly complicated its removal. When first seen, it was exceedingly fragile—little more than dust (Pl. xxviii c). It had to be brushed carefully and treated several times with weak solutions of vinyl acetate before it could be moved. Despite its great fragility, however, about 112 square inches were recovered, not all in one piece, it is true, but in several good-sized ones. Subsequent to field treatment, the specimens were further cleaned and mounted between glass.

That the fabric was in two layers in some places suggests the specimen was a bag, perhaps similar to present-day Ojibwa and Menominee bags. No painted or coloured decoration was discernible, nor was any design woven into the article. The material in the thread was charred beyond identification.

The technique used in the manufacture of this textile was what is called the "twined weave." The warp is a fairly coarse, two-ply thread set at about fourteen threads to the inch. The weft was a much finer, though still two-ply, thread which was worked across the warp in pairs with about ¼ inch between each pair. As in most twined weaving, the pairs of weft threads enclosed two warp threads at a time, were twisted around each other, enclosed another pair of warp threads, and so on across the width of the material. In this fabric, the pairs of warp threads enclosed by the wefts alternated in each row, so that if the warp threads were lettered A, B, C, D, E, F, etc., A and B, C and D, E and F would be together in the first row, but in the next B and C, D and E, etc., would be combined. With the third row of wefts the original combination would be resumed. This method of weaving always produces a fairly open fabric with the warp threads running on zigzag lines (Fig. 30, A).

The twined weave technique has been reported from many

parts of the world,* but so far as the writer is aware, never before from the Huron Indians. Its presence among them, however, is not surprising, for it is well known that other Iroquois-speaking peoples employed it. Several Mohawk burden-straps and a prisoners' halter of moose-hair are in existence†; and there is in the Royal Ontario Museum of Archaeology a very fine bag, said to have been a wampum pouch, from the Six Nations Indians, made of elm (?) bark and wool, woven very similarly to the specimen under consideration. Going farther afield, the modern Menominee use the technique, to mention but one people. On the archaeological side, Holmes describes, in his "Prehistoric Textile Art" and in "Prehistoric Textile Fabrics," what appear to be exact parallels from rock-shelters in Tennessee.‡

The *Jesuit Relations* imply that the Hurons wove, and refer twice to "hemp" as the material used. Le Jeune's Journal of 1637, for instance, speaks of Huron women using hemp,§ and Jérôme Lalemant, refers to a Huron "magician" who "ordered that no one should go to gather hemp" (that was the time when they usually go to the untilled plains, in order to gather a certain wild plant, from which twine for their nets is made)."‖ In the time of Lewis Morgan, the New York Iroquois were using slippery elm bark for thread. The treatment and manufacture of the raw material into thread, as described by Morgan,** was probably the same among Huron and Five Nations Indians.

*C. C. Willoughby, "Twined Weaving" (in Notes and News) (*American Anthropologist* n.s., vol. III, no. 1, p. 201-2).

†W. C. Orchard, "Mohawk Burden Straps" (*Indian Notes*, vol. VI, no. 4, Oct., 1929, p. 351-9); C. C. Willoughby, "Mohawk (Caughnawaga) Halter for Leading Captives" (*American Anthropologist*, n.s., vol. 40, no. 1, 1938, 49-50).

‡W. H. Holmes, "Prehistoric Textile Art of the Eastern United States" (Smithsonian Institution, *13th Annual Report of the Bureau of Ethnology for 1891-2*, Washington, 1896, pp. 3-46, and Plate III; "Prehistoric Textile Fabrics of the United States" (Smithsonian Institution, *3rd Annual Report of the Bureau of Ethnology for 1881*, Washington, 1884, p. 414).

§*Jesuit Relations*, vol. IX, p. 255.

‖*Ibid.*, vol. XXIII, p. 55. See also note 2, p. 325.

**L. H. Morgan, "Report on the Fabrics, Inventions, Implements and Utensils of the Iroquois" (University of New York, Appendix to report of regents on State Cabinet of Natural History and the Historical and Antiquarian Collection, 1851, pp. 84-7).

MISCELLANEOUS SPECIMENS

(a) Vegetable Remains

While most of the facts referred to in this section have been mentioned in other connections in this Report, it will be interesting to bring them together here to give the reader a concrete impression of the nature and extent of the vegetable remains. Both modern and ancient remains were found, and occasionally it was difficult to date a given piece. Modern material, aside from surface and near-surface finds, was noticeably common in the south end of the U-Trench, and in the southwest bastion. Partially charred wood, found not far from the surface in the central ditch of the moat, presented a problem: it appeared to have been brought there and, judging from the Indian pottery found on or near it, was used by Indians subsequently, one would suppose, to the destruction of the fort. On the other hand, it was isolated from other material of its kind.

When the establishment was burned on that ominous May 15, 1649, fairly large amounts of the wooden structures were charred or carbonized more or less completely, and so preserved. The sills along the west side of the Residence and the Chapel have already been referred to, as well as the large areas of plank flooring around the double fireplace, the west side and north end of the Residence, and part of the northwest bastion. Fragments of flooring also remained in the corners of each of the other bastions, and charred boards lying inside the east curtain indicated that there had once been a floor or boardwalk there, perhaps in the form of a sentry-walk. Inside the same curtain, the charred ends of stakes which had once supported its inner face were found in considerable numbers. Niches in the inside of the north curtain still retained the stumps of charred beams. Samples of most of this material were kept in the hope that it would be useful in tree-ring dating. Most of the charred wood was apparently cedar, or at any rate a softwood.

Just as there were quantities of charred wood, so also there was a good deal of naturally preserved wood. Most, if not all, of it appeared to be cedar; and according to the moisture content of the soil where it happened to be buried it was better or worse preserved. The doorstep in the southwest bastion, already referred to, had suffered a very great deal, being subject to seasonal wetting and drying, and probably owed its preservation to the presence of so much mortar round about it. The stakes in the root cellar were likewise poorly preserved; even the largest of the corner posts was soft. It was a very different matter however with the stakes in the refuse pit, which because of their constant immersion in wet blue clay were exceedingly well preserved. Comparably well preserved were a stake from a depth of nearly 7 feet in the central ditch and the sill under the northwest bastion. A cut was made to examine the substructure and what appeared to be an oaken beam beneath the masonry was surprisingly hard and sound. Isolated pieces of wood were found walling the central ditch and in some of the "trench fills" at the south end. They are indicated on the plan of these soil features.

So far as could be determined, the only pieces of non-structural wood to survive were the box, or box-like object, found in the fill in front of the central fireplace, and portions of charred hardwood handles which still remained in the sockets of several axes and the hammer.

A few fragments of birch-bark were found, chiefly inside the limits of the Chapel; there was no means of telling whether they were the remains of baskets or boxes.

The storage pit contained great quantities of vegetable remains, consolidated into a compact layer about 3 inches deep over the area. Around the edge the depth was about twice as great. A generous amount of this material was brought away for analysis, and submitted to Dr. H. B. Sifton, of the Department of Botany in the University of Toronto. Dr. Sifton reported that the mass was almost entirely of vegetable origin, and had not been ingested. Much of it had disintegrated too far to be identifiable, but the following seeds and fibres were isolated: hawthorne (Craetagus sp.), wild grape (Vitis sp.), blackberry (probably Rubus allegheniensis Porter), strawberry (Fragaris sp.), pin cherry (Prunus pennsylvanica L.), and fragments of cedar wood (Thuja occidentalis L.).

Thousands of squash seeds were embedded in the deep layer

adjacent to the stakes in sidewalls; in fact, they constituted almost its entire mass. The variety could not be determined with certainty, but was most likely aboriginal. A few pits of the wild plum were also recovered.

Other parts of the excavation yielded small quantities of maize and beans in charred condition, enough to indicate their importance in the economy of the place. They were localized chiefly along the west side of the Residence in front of the hearth and at the northeast corner of the hearth; small quantities were found on the floor of the Chapel.[*] A few corms in a charred state were found on the west side of the west moat, nearly opposite the juncture of Chapel and Residence. Dr. Sifton has suggested that these may be onions or some related plant. One charred acorn was found, but being a solitary specimen, was probably of no significance.

Small amounts of vegetable remains, including small seeds, were embedded in the material in the refuse pit, but no species not present elsewhere on the site were noticeable.

It is noteworthy that all species and varieties so far identified were of New World origin. The corn undoubtedly was, and the beans and squash almost as certainly are. There are no Old World species whatever, unless the onions were, nor does there appear to be any written record of attempted cultivation of such at Ste Marie.[†]

(b) Brick and Brick-like Material

Immense quantities of burnt clay of brick-like consistency were found along the west side of the compound, and in the area of the Residence and the Chapel generally. This clay was especially abundant over the west sill, on which it attained a depth of more than a foot immediately south of the northwest bastion. Great concentrations were also present around the fireplaces; it practically covered the Chapel fireplace, and at the southeast corner of the central fireplace it lay at least two feet thick at one point. Small quantities were scattered over all the above-mentioned areas, being perhaps more abundant over the Chapel than

[*]They were found principally in Squares 75K^1, 75M^1, 77O^1, 79M^1, 81K^1, and 83M^1.

[†]R. M. Saunders, "The First Introduction of European Plants and Animals into Canada" (*Canadian Historical Review*, vol. XVI, 1935, p. 401).

over the Residence. Four or five barrels of the larger fragments were collected but this was a mere fraction of the total. Pieces of exceptional size or quality were bagged. The material was a local clay burnt to a buff colour; along cleavage lines it frequently showed striations as if the raw clay had been mixed with straw or grass as a binder. Almost no flat surfaces appeared, and when they did were apparently accidental.

One large piece from 74P[1] did have a flat surface; in fact it had two, one of which was plain and the other showed a faint impression of closely woven textile. The thickness of this piece was 2½ inches.

It was suggested that the wooden buildings, and particularly their outside walls, were chinked with clay. The roof of the Chapel may have been similarly prepared, thus accounting for the presence of the material over its area. If the daub thus applied did not dry to its brick-like hardness naturally, it would at least be reduced to its present condition by the heat of the fire.

Enough fragments of true brick were found to enable four moderately large pieces to be put together, although none was complete. Most of them were found at the southeast corner of the central fireplace and the refuse pit near by, with another concentration near the well. As reconstructed, the bricks were nearly rectangular (although one shows an obtuse angle), flat-surfaced, and about 1½ inches thick, 4½ inches wide, and at least 5½ inches long. They were not mould made, however, and no two had exactly the same dimensions. The material in them is thought not to be a local clay and it was fired to an extremely hard consistency, like that in fire-bricks. They must have been specially imported for some specific use, which we cannot now determine (Fig. 24, B, and Pl. xxvii b).

The presence in quantity of mortar and other material of European derivation, has been mentioned above.

IV. Summary

THE direct results of excavation at Ste Marie I may be summarized under the following headings: (1) the uncovering of the outlines of buildings; (2) the recovery of details of construction; (3) the recovery of artifacts of European origin; and (4) the recovery of artifacts of Indian origin. The first is perhaps the most obvious result, and was certainly a leading motive in undertaking the work. It was accomplished with a good measure of success, although in certain spots disturbance in recent times had blurred the evidence, as, for instance, in the vicinity of the southwest bastion. As for details of construction, much information was obtained such as that concerning masonry and woodwork, types of material used, and kinds of hardware employed. A great number of artifacts of European origin were recovered, including iron goods of many kinds, copper objects, some silver, glass, tableware, hooks and eyes, ornaments, and a dozen other items. The collection of tools, especially those used by carpenters and masons, was large and diversified. Aboriginal artifacts were less numerous, though by no means scarce; they included pottery, bone, antler, and stone objects.

The indirect results of the excavation are naturally more numerous and more difficult to assess. The acquisition of sufficient data to enable reconstruction to be undertaken must, from many standpoints, be considered the most important. It was indeed the primary objective of the work. Details of the ground plan, of masonry and carpentry work, dimensions of buildings, types of hardware employed, all contribute materially to this end. Unfortunately, owing to the conflagration which destroyed the establishment, there was but little woodwork remaining from which to derive clues as to the type of superstructure, placement and size of openings, style of decoration (if any), and a thousand other details concerning which information would have been most welcome. For these, it will be necessary to consult library sources and whatever French-Canadian architecture of the period may still be extant. Even at best, the exact nature of the wooden superstructure must remain in some doubt; only the height of the chimney could be ascertained from the ruins with any degree of accuracy. At any rate, data recovered concerning this complex of buildings at Ste Marie I has added much to our knowledge of French building procedure in Canada at that time, such as the sizes and shapes which were deemed most advantageous, the materials and tools used, and many other details.

The excavation may perhaps claim to have made some contribution to historical knowledge. Ste Marie I, long regarded as an important episode in Canadian history, and even of considerable continental significance, was never before known in such intimate detail. Matters which were but recently the subject of speculation are now reduced to concrete fact. The interior buildings are specifically known and located, and their size and placement are no longer open to conjecture. Moreover, the very utensils which were used by the priests, the brothers, the blacksmith, and the carpenters may now be seen, and studied—a fact which will greatly aid the student of the period in reconstructing the scene accurately and with confidence.

The collection of artifacts, especially those of European origin, is outstanding for the period, and may long remain so. Comprehensive enough in regard to tools of known use, the collection also contains a great number of pieces, especially of metal, whose purposes at the present time can only be guessed. Moreover, it embraces a number of specimens of considerable artistic merit, and at least one of singular beauty. The aboriginal specimens throw a good deal of light on native arts and crafts of the time, although Ste Marie itself was never an Indian site. What artifacts were found on it were either bought by the French from the Indians for their own use, or dropped there by visiting Indians previous to, during, or after the French occupation. Since almost all appear to be of Huron origin, it is assumed that only those of evident Algonkian derivation date from the post-occupation period, though the total amount of Indian material is relatively small, it will be useful in establishing a datum line for a chronology of the aboriginal archaeology of the region. In the same connection, samples of wood and charcoal obtained from the site have been saved, in the hope that from them it will be possible to work out a tree-ring chronology for the Huron area. Their value in this regard is enhanced by the fact that they carry us back directly a full three hundred years, and are well authenticated. It has not been possible to include an analysis of the bone material from the site, but when the work has been completed, it is hoped to make it the subject of a supplementary report.

V. Appendices

Copy of the description of the site of Fort Ste Marie, from the manuscript, "Voyages et Recherches" by the Reverend Félix Martin, S. J., written in 1855, pp. 64-7.

Le Fort Ste. Marie. Le Fort Ste. Marie est placé sur le 16e lot, de la 3e concession du township de Tay. Aujourd'hui ce sol est tellement couvert par la forêt, qu'il est impossible d'apercevoir le fort en abordant au rivage dont il n'est éloigné cependant que de cinquante pieds.

Nous nous occupâmes aussitôt à lever le plan de terre et à nous assurer de sa position. En dégageant les fondations des débris qui les couvrent, il était facile d'en suivre les traces et de les mesurer.

Le fort est construit en bonne maçonnerie de pierre et de chaux et les ruines s'élèvent encore de deux à quatre pieds au dessus du sol. Le travail, très bien exécuté, suppose évidemment des ouvriers de profession. On ne trouve pas de pierres dans les environs, et la necessité d'aller les chercher ailleurs avec si peu de ressources à cette époque pour les transporter, a dû augmenter beaucoup la difficulté.

Le fort est une parallélogramme allongée, flanqué de bastions à ses angles. Malgré les irrégularités qui se trouvent dans les détails de cette construction, et dont il est difficile aujourd'hui de s'expliquer tous les motifs, on reconnait sans peine dans ce travail des notions d'art militaire, appliquées avec soin.

Deux côtés seulement ont une enceinte continuée et une courtine complète. La courtine de l'est, qui fait face à la campagne, semble interrompue au milieu d'une manière régulière qui permet de croire que la porte d'entrée devait se trouver là. Le bastion B (S.E.), entièrement fermé, ne laisse voir à la hauteur du sol aucune trace d'ouverture. Mais comme le pied du mur doit avoir plongé dans le fossé, il est possible que la porte était placée au dessus des ruines qui existent aujourd'hui.

Les deux courtines de l'ouest et du sud n'existent plus. Il n'y reste pas de trace de maçonnerie et par plusieurs excavations nous avons pu constater qu'il ne s'y trouve aucune fondation solide. Il est à présumer qu'il le consistait en de fortes palissades. C'était suffisant en effet pour défendre l'approche de ces deux côtes, où il y avait de moins à craindre. Il règne en avant des deux bastions C (N O) et D (S O), et à leurs pieds un fossé assez profond qui protégeait la courtine, et qu'on distingue très sensiblement aujourd'hui.

Le bastion C (N O) plus petit que les deux premiers, offre cette singularité que son flanc sud, formé d'un mur plus large que les autres côtés, s'avance beaucoup dans l'interieur du fort, et a une tête très régulière. Une excavation pratiquée à ce point nous a fait découvrir, à deux pieds environs de profondeur le lit d'une fondation et les traces d'un plancher brûlé; nous y avons trouvé aussi de grands clous à plancheier, des os de castor et un morceau de cuivre, qui pouvait avoir appartenu à quelque ustensile de ménage.

Le bastion D (S O) est plus petit encore que le bastion C (N O); il est lié par un de ses angles avec une construction carrée E (S) qui formait peut-être la base d'une tour du haut de laquelle on pouvait voir au loin et surveiller les approches. L'irrégularité qui se manifeste en ce point devait tenir à quelque raison locale que nous ne connaissons pas aujourd'hui.

En avant des bastions D (S O) et B (S E), et dans la direction de la courtine qui les rejoint, règne un fossé très large et qui a dû être assez creux pour que l'eau de la rivière put s'y introduire. Il va en effet jusqu'à la rivière, après s'être incliné un peu vers l'ouest. Non seulement il servait à isoler le fort, mais il devait être comme un port et un abri pour les canots des sauvages voyageurs. En deux endroits il s'élargit en forme de basin régulier, pour rendre sans doute le débarquement plus facile.

De l'autre côté de cet espèce de canal, se voit un terrain assez vaste, défendu lui-même par une fossé en dehors, et un petit parapet en terre. Sa direction est encore très visible. Il partit du bastion B (S E), et suivant à peu près la forme d'une vaste lunette, il venait expirer à la rivière. Je croirais volontier que cette enceinte ne formait pas un simple ouvrage avancé pour protéger les approches du fort, mais qu'elle était destinée à offrir aux sauvages qui venaient quelquefois en si grand nombre visiter ce poste, un lieu favorable et sûr pour y dresser leurs cabanes.

Extract from the Autobiographie du Père Chaumonot, et la compagnie de Jésus et son complément, by the Reverend Père Félix Martin, 1885, p. 55.

Nos demeures sont d'écorce, comme celles des sauvages, sans divisions en salle, chambre, cuisine, cave, excepté pour la chapelle. La reste est en commune. Nous n'avons ni tables, ni bancs pour prendre les repas, ni vases ou verres pour boire le vin, l'eau ou autre liquide, ni écuelle, ni assiettes, ni entremets, ni dessert, ni portions, ni pain, ni fruits. Tous les ustensils de notre cuisine et de notre réfectoire consistent dans un grand plat d'écorce, rempli d'une certaine bouillie de farine de blé d'Inde, cuite avec quelques poissons séchés à la fumée. Voilà tout le sel qu'on y met. Je ne vois rien à quoi l'on puis mieux comparer cette (56) sagamité (c'est le nom que nous lui donnons) qu'à la colle qui sert à fixer la papier sur les murs . . . .

Notre lit se compose d'une écorce et d'une natte épaisse à peu près comme une piastre de Florence. Pour les drapes, on n'en parle pas, même pour les malades.

Ce qui nous incommode le plus est la fumée qui, faute de cheminée, remplit toute la cabane, et gâte tout ce que nous voudrions garder. Quand certains vents soufflent, la position est très pénible à cause de la douleur des yeux. Nous n'avons pas le soir, en hiver, d'autre lumière que celle du foyer, pour réciter notre bréviaire, étudier les préceptes de la langue ou autres travaux. Le jour, la lumière nous vient par l'ouverture pratiquée au sommet de la cabane, qui sert en même temps de cheminée et de fenêtre.

Voilà notre manière de vivre dans notre résidence . . . .

This extract which describes Chaumonot's impression of Ste Marie was likely written shortly after his arrival there. Father Jones on page 315 of *Old Huronia,* gives the date of his arrival at Ste Marie as September 10, 1639.

APPENDIX B

DIMENSIONS OF THE EUROPEAN COMPOUND AND ITS STRUCTURES

A. The Compound
  (a) From southwest corner of southwest bastion to northwest corner of northwest bastion . . . . . . 170′ 4″
  (b) From northwest corner of northwest bastion to northeast corner of northeast bastion . . . . . 94′ 0″
  (c) From northeast corner of northeast bastion to southeast corner of southeast bastion . . . . . . 182′ 2″
  (d) From southeast corner of southeast bastion to southwest corner of southwest bastion . . . . . . 75′ 0″
  (e) From west face of southeast bastion to southeast corner of southwest bastion . . . . 36′ 11″
B. The Southwest Bastion
  (a) Length of west wall . . . . 18′ 0″

(b) Length of north wall . . . . 15' 0"
(c) Length of east wall . . . . 17' 10"
(d) Length of south wall . . . . 15' 3"
(e) Height of wall above footing W   N   E   S

	W	N	E	S
(e) Height of wall above footing	4' 2"	3' 0"	4' 0"	4' 8"
(f) Thickness of footing	2' 11"	3' 0"	3' 2½"	2' 10½"
(g) Thickness of wall	2' 0"	2' 2"	2' 2"	2' 1"

C. The Southeast Bastion
  (a) Length of west wall . . . . 26' 7"
  (b) Length of north wall . . . . 22' 6"
  (c) Length of east wall . . . . 25' 11"
  (d) Length of south wall . . . . 22' 9"
  (e) Height of wall above footing W   N   E   S

	W	N	E	S
(e) Height of wall above footing	3'7"-2'10"	4' 3"-3'	3'3"-3'11"	0-3'6"
(f) Thickness of wall	2'3"	2'3"	2'3"	2'2"-2'4"
(g) Thickness of footing	3'2"	3'0"	2'10"	2'10"-3'

  (h) Height of threshold above footing, 5" or one course.

D. The Northeast Bastion

	W	N	E	S
(a) Length of walls	27'5"	22'0"	28'0"	21'10"
(b) Height of wall above footing	4'9"-3'4"	4'1"	3'10"-3'4"	4'9"-4'0"
(c) Thickness of wall	2'2"	2'3"	2'4"	2'3"
(d) Thickness of footing	2'11"	3'0"	3'1"	2'11"

  (e) Height of threshold above footing, 1' 7"
  (f) Distance between northwest corner and outer
      face of north curtain . . . . 10' 5"

E. The Northwest Bastion

	W	N	E	S
(a) Length of walls	19'0"	16'4"	7'6"	5'7"
(b) Height of walls	1'5"	2'0"	2'0"	2'8"
(c) Thickness of walls	1'10"	2'0"	1'7"	2'3"

  (d) Width of door . . . . 2'7"

F. The North Curtain
  (a) Length . . . . 56'8"
  (b) Width at west end . . . . 2'3"
  (c) Width at east end . . . . 2'3"
  (d) Height at west end . . . . 1'10"
  (e) Height above footing at northeast bastion . . . 3'4"

G. The East Curtain
  (a) Length (i.e., distance between southeast corner of north-
     east bastion and the northeast corner of the southeast
     bastion . . . . 127'11"

    (b) Length of north segment of arm . . . . 12'5"
    (c) Width of north segment . . . . 2'6"
    (d) Height of curtain at north end . . . . 1'5"
    (e) Width of curtain at north end . . . . 2'6"
    (f) Width of curtain at south end . . . . 2'6"

H. The Residence
    (a) Length — 55 feet.
    (b) Width — 30 feet (?)

J. The Chapel
    (a) Length — 40 feet.
    (b) Width — 20 feet.

K. Double Fireplace
    (a) Length — 7½ to 8¼ feet.
    (b) Width — 7¼ feet.

L. Central Fireplace
    (a) Length, overall — 11¾ feet.
    (b) Width — 6½ feet.
    (c) Hearth — 9½ feet long x 5 feet wide.
    (d) Accessory Wall — 7 feet.

M. Chapel Fireplace
    (a) Length, overall — 14½ feet.
    (b) Width — 5 feet.
    (c) Hearth — 12¼ feet x 3¼ feet.

N. Storage Pit
    (a) Dimensions — 8½ x 8½ feet.

O. Refuse Pit
    (a) Dimensions — 6 feet x 9 feet.

P. Well
    (a) Diameter — 5 feet.

APPENDIX C

THE GALBRAITH PLAN

After the above account was written, Mr. John S. Galbraith of Toronto kindly loaned to the author a pencilled diary made in 1878 by his father, containing a sketch plan of the site of Ste Marie I. This plan, drawn in two parts, one to show the layout of the European compound, the other of the Indian compound, is here reproduced in photostatic copy by the kind permission of Mr. Galbraith. The diary accompanying the map pertains to a canoe trip in Georgian Bay and is written in Ojibwa, except for the map itself which is annotated in

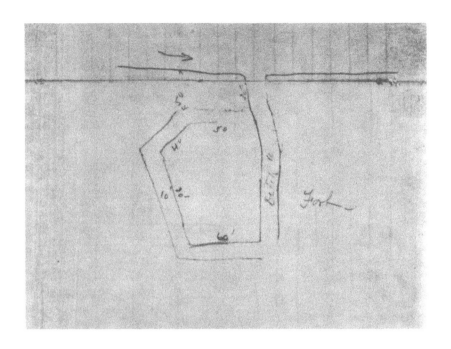

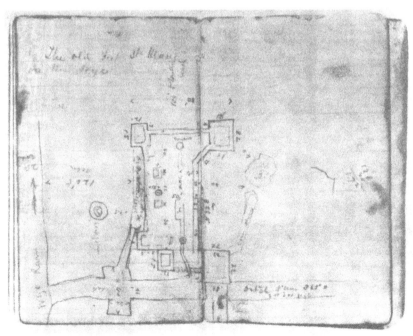

MAP. 11. Plan of Ste Marie I drawn in 1878 by Professor Galbraith, photostatic copy reproduced by courtesy of Mr. John S. Galbraith.

English. It is the only one of the early maps which shows detailed dimensions, and most of the features have been indicated with remarkable accuracy. Angles of orientation are also carefully indicated.

From this plan, it is apparent that in 1878 the earth-works of the Indian compound were still visible. As recorded by Galbraith and Hallen they extended south of the moat, meeting at an angle on the south side. The west side was even then indefinite, however. Neither plan agrees well with Burnet's, in so far as this area is concerned.

The plan of the European compound is shown in surprising detail. The general outlines are correct, and the shape and placement of the bastions are right. There is some error in the size of the north bastions, for all are slightly larger than shown. A conspicuous feature here is that for the first time, the bastions are shown correctly as rectangular, and not as quadrilaterals of various forms as on earlier plans. Even more important is the rectangular structure adjacent to the southwest bastion at its northwest corner. This is Martin's Bastion D. Although only a vestige of this structure remained at the time of excavation (Wall Fragment 1), these four early plans point definitely to its existence in the original fortification. Galbraith gives its length as 8 feet, 5 inches on the south side, and on the west 8 feet; these are the only dimensions given for it in any source. The existence of a structure where the south or double fireplace stood is shown, and the central fireplace in the Residence is so clearly indicated that it appears as if Galbraith was aware of the function of what must at that time have been a heap of rubble. On the other hand, the Chapel fireplace is not even hinted at.

The two concave depressions which proved to be a refuse pit and a storage pit are marked "W," and presumably were regarded by Galbraith as wells. The well at the north end of the compound is marked "new well," on what authority is not known. The central ditch is marked, as is also the ditch at the west side.

The main moat with an indicated breadth of 10 feet is shown as passing the fortification and continuing "2 or 300 feet" to the east. The ditch on the west side cuts southwestward to empty into the one turning basin, which appears as a large rectangle somewhat west of the fortifications.

Many minor details are also recorded, such as a heap of stones in the field near the river, and the loose stones east of the fortifications. This plan is undoubtedly the most accurate, the most detailed, and the least influenced by preconceived ideas that was made prior to excavation.

VI. Bibliography

THE bibliography which follows includes textual references and essential material. It does not, on the other hand, contain by any means all of the sources which have been examined, or are known to exist. It lists primary material like *The Jesuit Relations,* and Sagard's *Long Voyage,* supplementary material, such as Hunt's *Wars of the Iroquois,* and a number of references to anthropological and geological literature. Articles presenting the results of recent historical and scientific research, such as Saunders's *First Introduction of European Plants* and Jury's *Fairfield on the Thames* are pertinent to the subject material and are therefore included here. Finally, an attempt has been made to give references to material on some of the problems raised by the excavation, such as glass, firearms, and medals. It should be emphasized, however, that the bibliography is in no respect complete, but aims merely to provide background material for the study of the site and the problems it raises.

Anonymous. "Early mission sites." With illustrations of crosses, medals, and rings. Rochester Museum of Arts and Sciences (*Museum service,* vol. IX, no. 4, Apr., 1936, p. 60).

—— "History of the Shrine properties" (*Martyrs' shrine message,* vol. VI, no. 4, Dec., 1942, pp. 7, 21).

—— Ste. Marie in the Relations: A summary. Manuscript in the possession of the Jesuit Order, n.d. Pp. 17.

BAIN, JAMES, JR. "The present condition of the old Fort at Ste. Marie" (Canadian Institute, *Proceedings,* 3rd series, vol. III, 1884-5, Toronto, 1886, p. 278-79).

BARBEAU, C. MARIUS. "The house that Mac built" (*Beaver,* outfit 276, Dec., 1945, pp. 10-13).

BRESSANI, FRANCESCO GIUSEPPE. *Relation abrégée de quelques missions des pères de la Compagnie de Jésus dans la Nouvelle-France; traduite de l'italien et augmentée d'un avant-propos, de la biographie de l'auteur, et d'un grand nombre de notes et de gravures, par F. Martin.* Montreal: Lovell, 1852. Pp. 336.

Canadian Institute. "Report of the historical section" (*Transactions,* vol. III, 1891-2, Toronto, 1893, p. 59-61).

CHAMPLAIN, SAMUEL DE. *Voyages and discoveries made in New France, from the year 1615 to the end of the year 1618, etc.*

Translated and edited by H. H. Langton and W. F. Ganong. Vol. III in "The Works of Samuel de Champlain." Toronto: Champlain Society, 1929. Pp. xvi, 418.

CHAPMAN, L. J. and PUTNAM, D. F. "The physiography of south-central Ontario" (*Scientific agriculture,* vol. XVI, 1936, pp. 457-77).

—— "The soils of south-central Ontario" (*Scientific agriculture,* vol. XVIII, no. 4, 1937, pp. 161-97).

CHASTELAIN, PIERRE. *Affectus amantis Christum Jesum, seu exercitium amoris erga Dominum Jesum oro tota hebdomada, auctore P. Petro Chastelain.* . . . Parisiis, apud D. Bechat, 1648.

COPWAY, GEORGE. *The traditional history and characteristic sketches of the Ojibway Nation.* Boston: Benjamin B. Mussey, 1851. Pp. x, 266.

COYNE, JAMES H. "The Jesuits' mill or mortar: The great dispersion of the Hurons, 1649-51" (Royal Society of Canada, *Transactions,* sec. II, 1926, pp. 9-14).

DEVINE, E. J. *Old Fort Ste. Marie: Home of the Canadian martyrs, 1639-49.* 2nd ed. Fort Ste. Marie. Martyrs' Shrine, Midland, n.d. Pp. 60.

DILLON, EDWARD. *Glass.* London: Methuen, 1907. Pp. xxviii, 374.

GOLDTHWAIT, JAMES W. *An instrumental survey of the shore-line of the extinct lakes Algonquin and Nipissing in southwestern Ontario.* Canada, Geological Survey, memoir 10. Ottawa: King's Printer, 1910. Pp. 57.

GREENER, W. W. *The gun and its development with notes on shooting.* 3rd ed. London, Paris, New York, and Melbourne: Cassell, 1885. Pp. 768.

HARRIS, WM. R. *History of the early missions in western Canada.* Toronto: Hunter Rose, 1893. Pp. 339.

HOLMES, WILLIAM H. "Prehistoric textile art of the eastern United States" (Smithsonian Institution, Bureau of American Ethnology, *13th annual report for 1891-2,* Washington, 1896, pp. 3-46).

—— "Prehistoric textile fabrics of the United States, derived from impressions on pottery" (Smithsonian Institution, Bureau of American Ethnology, *3rd annual report for 1881,* Washington, 1884, pp. 397-425).

HUNT, GEORGE T. *The wars of the Iroquois: A study in intertribal trade relations.* Madison: University of Wisconsin Press, 1940. Pp. 209.

HUNTER, ANDREW F. "French relics from village sites of the Hurons:

The geographical distribution of these relics in the counties of Simcoe, York and Ontario." Canadian Institute, *3rd annual report*, session 1888-9; being part of appendix to the Report of the Minister of Education, Ontario, 1889. Toronto: Warwick Bros. and Rutter, 1889, pp. 42-6.

—— *A history of Simcoe county*. 2 vols. Barrie. Printed by the County Council, 1909.

JEFFERYS, CHARLES W. "The reconstruction of the Port Royal habitation of 1605-13" (*Canadian historical review*, vol. XX, no. 4, Dec., 1939, pp. 369-77).

JENNESS, D. *The Indians of Canada*. Department of Mines, National Museum of Canada, Bulletin 65. Ottawa: King's Printer, 1932. Pp. x, 446.

The Jesuit Relations and Allied Documents. Travels and explorations of the Jesuit missionaries of New France, 1610-1791. The original French, Latin, and Italian texts, with English translations and notes; illustrated with portraits, maps, and facsimiles. Edited by R. G. Thwaites. 73 vols. Cleveland: Burrows Brothers, 1896-1901.

JONES, ARTHUR E. " 'Wendake Ehen,' or Old Huronia" (Bureau of Archives for the Province of Ontario, *Fifth Report*, 1908, Toronto: King's Printer, 1909. XXXIII pp. 1-505).

JURY, WILFRID. *Fairfield on the Thames: Report of excavations made on the site of the early mission village, 1942-43 by Wilfrid Jury.* University of Western Ontario, Bulletin of the Museums, nos. 3-5, 1945-48.

—— "Old Fairfield on the Thames" (*Canadian historical review*, vol. XXV, no. 4, Dec., 1944, pp. 409-16).

KINEITZ, W. VERNON. *The Indians of the western great lakes, 1615-1760.* Museum of Anthropology of the University of Michigan, occasional contributions, no. 10. Ann Arbor: University of Michigan Press, 1940. Pp. xiv, 427.

LAVERDIÈRE, CHARLES H. and CASGRAIN, H.-R. *Le journal des Jésuites; publié d'après le manuscrit original conservé aux archives du Séminaire de Québec.* Deuxième édition, exactement conformé à la première (1871). Montréal: Chez J.-M. Valois, 1892. Pp. 403.

LEVERETT, F. and TAYLOR, F. B. *The pleistocene of Indiana and Michigan and the history of the Great Lakes.* United States Geological Survey monograph 53, 1915. Pp. 529.

McCOY, JAMES C. *Jesuit Relations of Canada, 1632-1673: A bibliography.* With an introduction by Lawrence C. Wroth. Paris: Arthur Rau, 1937. Pp. xvi, 346.

MARTIN, FÉLIX. *Autobiographie du Père Chaumonot, de la compagnie de Jésus et son complément.* Paris: H. Oudin, 1885. Pp. x, 291.

—— *Huron et Iroquois: Le P. Jean de Brébeuf, sa vie, ses travaux, son martyre.* Collection Saint-Michel. Paris: G. Tequi, 1882. Pp. vi, 298.

—— *The life of Father Isaac Jogues, missionary priest of the Society of Jesus, slain by the Mohawk Iroquois in the present state of New York, Oct. 18, 1646.* Translated from the French by John Gilmary Shea. New York, Cincinnati, and St. Louis: Benziger Bros., 1885. Pp. 263.

—— Voyages et recherches dans l'ancien pays des Hurons. Par le Rév. Père Félix Martin, S. J., en 1855. Manuscript in the Archives of Collège Sainte-Marie. Montréal.

MAYER, JOSEPH R. *Flintlocks of the Iroquois, 1620-1687.* Rochester Museum of Arts and Sciences, Research Records, no. 6, 1943. Pp. 59.

MERCER, H. C. *Ancient carpenters' tools: Illustrated and explained together with the implements of the lumberman, joiner and cabinet maker, in use in the eighteenth century.* Doylestown, Pa.: Bucks County Historical Society, 1929. Pp. x, 328.

MORGAN, LEWIS H. "Report on the fabrics, inventions, implements and utensils of the Iroquois, made to the Regents of the University, Jan. 22, 1851" (University of New York, Appendix to the *Fourth annual report of the regents on the condition of the State Cabinet of Natural History and the historical and antiquarian collection.* Albany: Charles van Renthuysen, 1851, pp. 67-117).

Ontario archaeological report, 1899: Being part of appendix to the report of the minister of education, Ontario (Toronto: Warwick Bros. and Rutter, 1900, pp. 1-200).

ORCHARD, WILLIAM C. "Mohawk burden straps" (*Indian notes,* vol. VI, no. 4, Oct., 1929, pp. 351-9).

OSBORNE, A. C. "Old Penetanguishene: Sketches of its pioneer, naval and military days" (Simcoe County Pioneer and Historical Society, *Pioneer papers,* no. 5, 1912, pp. 1-82).

(PAQUIN, J.) *The tragedy of Old Huronia (Wendake Ehen). By a pilgrim. A popular story of the Jesuit Huron missions of Canada. 1615-1650.* Fort Ste Marie, Ont. Martyrs' Shrine, Midland. 1932. Pp. xvi, 282.

PARKMAN, FRANCIS. *The Jesuits in North America in the seventeenth century.* Boston: Little, Brown, 1889. Pp. xcii, 463.

QUIMBY, GEORGE I., JR. "European trade articles as chronological indicators for the archaeology of the historic period in Michigan" (Michigan Academy of Science, Arts and Letters, *Papers for 1938*, vol. XXIV, part 4, 1939, pp. 25-31).

ROCHEMONTEIX, CAMILLE DE. *Les Jésuites et la Nouvelle-France au XVIIe siècle: D'après beaucoup de documents inédits.* Vol. I. Paris: Letouzey et Ané, 1895. Pp. 488.

SAGARD-THÉODAT, GABRIEL. "Le grand voyage au pays des Hurons, situé en Amerique vers la mer douce, aux derniers confins de la Nouvelle France, dite Canada" (In *Trois Voyages au Canada: Jacques Cartier, 1534 et 1536; Samuel de Champlain, 1608 et 1611; et Frère Gabriel Sagard, 1624.* Collection Voyages et Découvertes, Paris: Aux Editions Carrefour, n.d., pp. 1-234).

SAUNDERS, R. M. "The first introduction of European plants and animals into Canada" (*Canadian historical review*, vol. XVI, no. 4, Dec., 1935, pp. 388-406).

SPECK, FRANK G. "Notes on the material culture of the Huron" (*American anthropologist*, vol. XIII, no. 2, n.s., Apr.-June, 1911, pp. 208-28).

STANLEY, G. M. "Lower Algonquin beaches of Cape Rich, Georgian Bay" (Geological Society of America, *Bulletin*, vol. XLVIII, Nov. 1, 1937, pp. 1665-86).

—— "Lower Algonquin beaches of Penetanguishene peninsula" (Geological Society of America, *Bulletin*, vol. XLVII, Dec. 31, 1936, pp. 1933-60).

WILLOUGHBY, C. C. "A Mohawk (Caughnawaga) halter for leading captives" (*American anthropologist*, vol. XL, no. 1, n.s., Jan.-Mar., 1938, pp. 49-50).

—— "Twined weaving [in Notes and News]" (*American anthropologist*, vol. III, no. 1, n.s., Jan.-Mar., 1901, pp. 201-2).

WINTEMBERG, W. J. "Distinguishing characteristics of Algonkian and Iroquoian cultures" (Canada: Dept. of Mines, National Museum of Canada, Bulletin 67, *Annual report for 1929*, Ottawa: King's Printer, 1931, pp. 65-126).

—— "The Sidey-Mackay village site" (*American antiquity*, vol. XI, no. 3, Jan., 1946, pp. 154-82).

WROTH, LAWRENCE C. *The Jesuit relations from New France* (Reprint from papers of the Bibliographical Society of America, 1936, vol. XXX, part 2, pp. 149).

INDEX

Index

PLATES

PLATE I

a. View of site from hill to north.

b. View of site from north and before excavation.

PLATE II

a. Test trench between river and compound (U-Trench).

b. Small cannon, originally brought to Ste Marie I, later taken to Ste Marie II, and found there in the present century. Now in Martyrs' Shrine Museum.

PLATE III

b. Post moulds along east side of Chapel.

a. Fragments of wooden sill in Residence.

PLATE IV

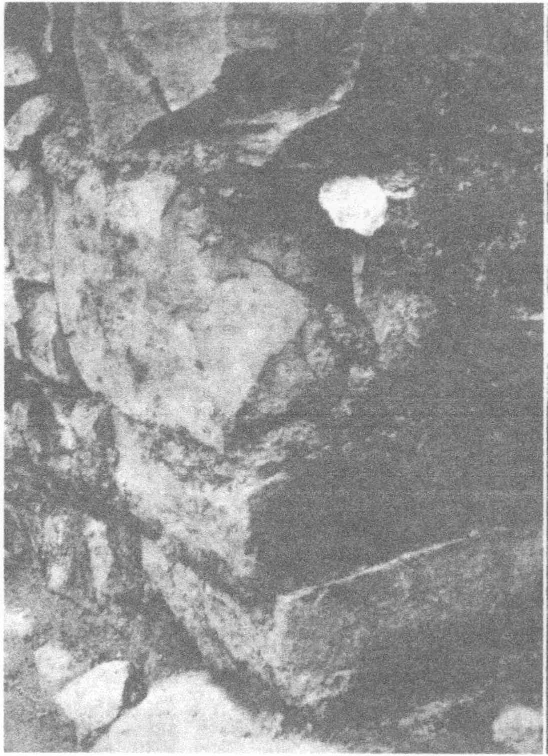

a. Detail of masonry at corner of southwest

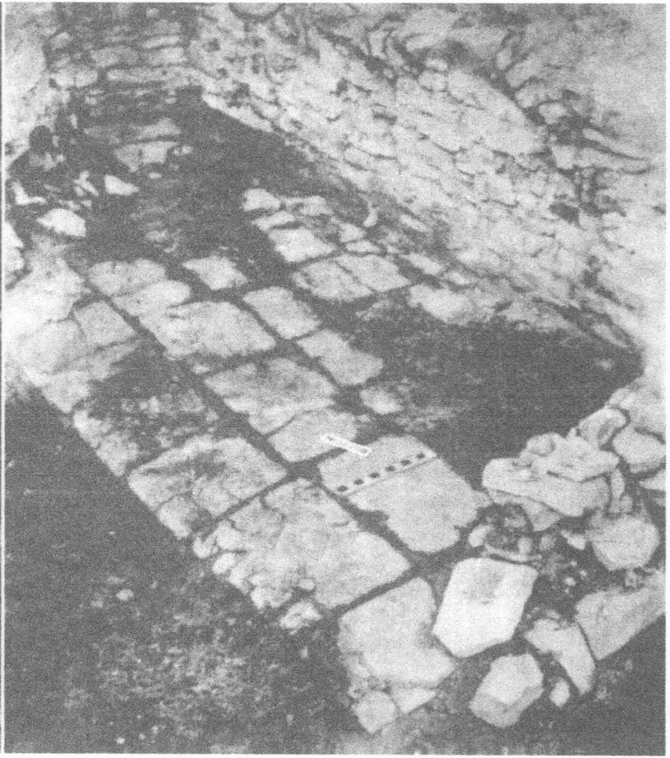

b. Central fireplace, almost completely excavated.

PLATE V

a. Refuse pit partly excavated.

b. Iron axe with charred handle, before removal.

PLATE VI

a. Wooden stakes from refuse pit.

b. Site of central fireplace before excavation. The monument is visible in later photographs also.

PLATE VII

a. Central fireplace from the west, after excavation. The small heap
of stones indicates the position of the cyst.

b. Wooden tray in position in the cyst.

PLATE VIII

a. Profile showing depth of stake moulds under sill of the Chapel.

b. View of west side of excavated compound, from Chapel fireplace.

PLATE IX

a. Storage pit partly excavated.

b. Storage pit excavated.

PLATE X

a. Fragment of Venetian glass in position in storage pit.

b. Chapel area looking north.

PLATE XI

a. Southwest bastion before excavation.

b. Southwest bastion completely cleared, looking north.

PLATE XII

a. Detail of north wall of southwest bastion.

b. Detail of threshold in southwest bastion.

PLATE XIII

a. Interior of north wall of southeast bastion.

b. View of northwest bastion from the north.

PLATE XIV

a. Charred boards north of Chapel fireplace.

b. North curtain after excavation.

PLATE XV

a. South corner of east curtain.

b. Inside face of east curtain showing charred retaining stakes.

PLATE XVI

a. View of false wall from the north.

b. Wall fragment 1, at southwest bastion.

PLATE XVII

a. Wall fragment 2, from the east.

b. Southwest corner of Residence showing foundation wall and double fireplace.

PLATE XVIII

a. Forge flue partly cleared.

b. Forge flue after excavation. Both views are from the south.

PLATE XIX

a. View of excavated central fireplace from the southeast, to show accessory wall and charred flooring.

b. Detail of exterior of chimney wall of central fireplace. Note the missing stone at the left.

PLATE XX

a. Stonefall from chimney of central fireplace.

b. View looking north over Chapel area, showing sill, charred timbers and stones. The north end of the Residence appears in the foreground.

PLATE XXI

a. The moat looking towards the Wye River.

b. Wood remains south of the storage pit.

PLATE XXII

a. Soil pattern between the two south bastions.

b. Profile of a trench fill.

PLATE XXIII

a. North end of compound looking east, after excavation.

b. Flat Rock Point, showing limestone outcropping.

PLATE XXIV

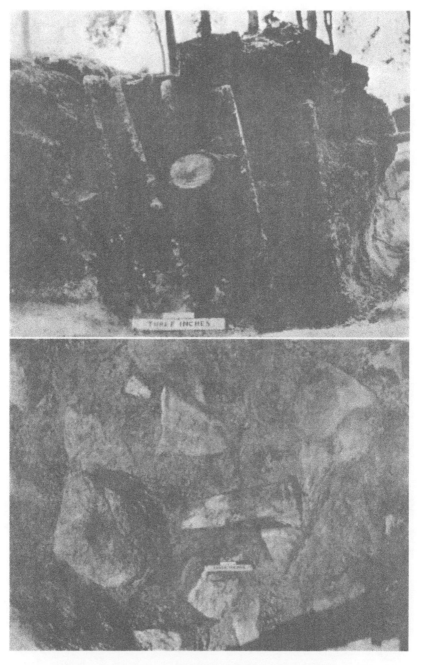

a. Five of the six angle irons in place in Residence sill.

b. Heavy iron wedge as found near the east curtain.

PLATE XXV

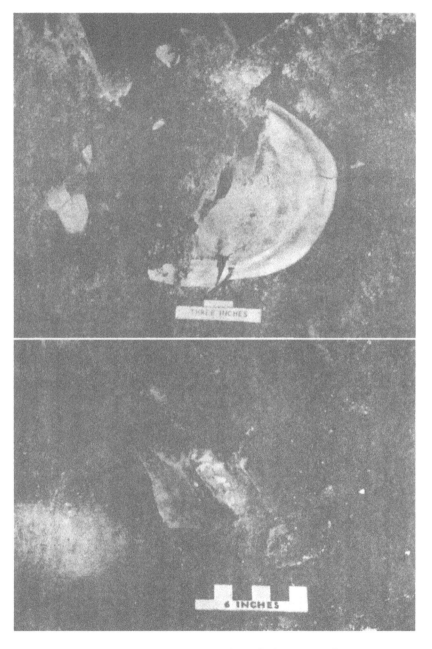

a. Fragmentary copper plate, before removal.

b. Iron hoe or shovel in position near the well.

PLATE XXVI

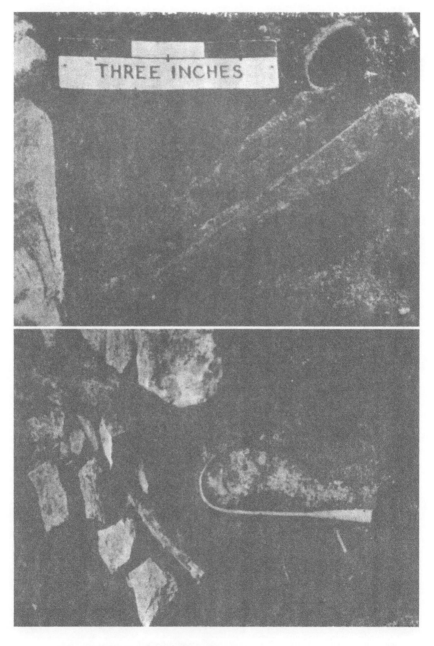

a. Part of sewing kit, as found.

b. Iron hook of unknown use, lying north of central fireplace.

PLATE XXVII

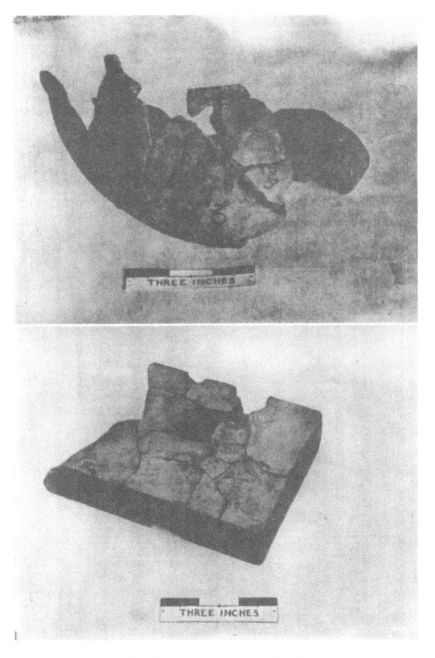

a. Clay vessel in European style, but of local manufacture.

b. Hard-baked brick, incomplete.

PLATE XXVIII

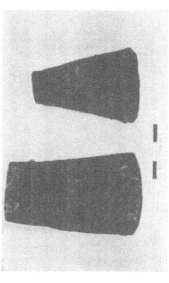

c. Fragment of textile before removal.

a. Two views of a granite axe, found above the Chapel fireplace.

b. Two iron axes: left, early American; right,

PLATE XXIX

d. Iron adze in position.

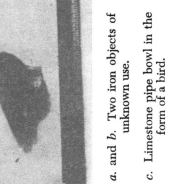

a. and *b.* Two iron objects of
unknown use.

c. Limestone pipe bowl in the
form of a bird.

PLATE XXX

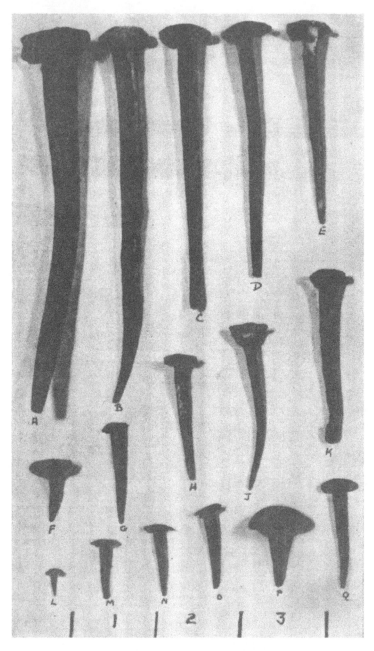

Iron nails and tacks of various styles.

PLATE XXXI

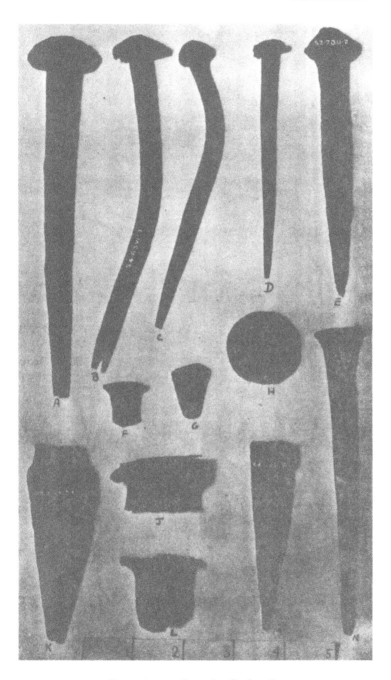

Large iron nails and spike heads.

PLATE XXXII

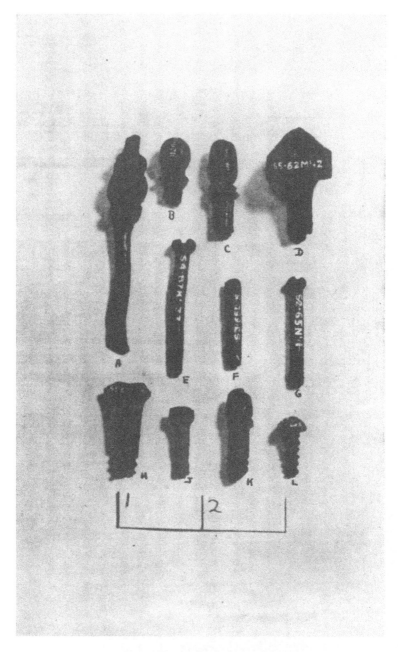

Ornamental iron nails, screw-nails and threaded nails.

PLATE XXXIII

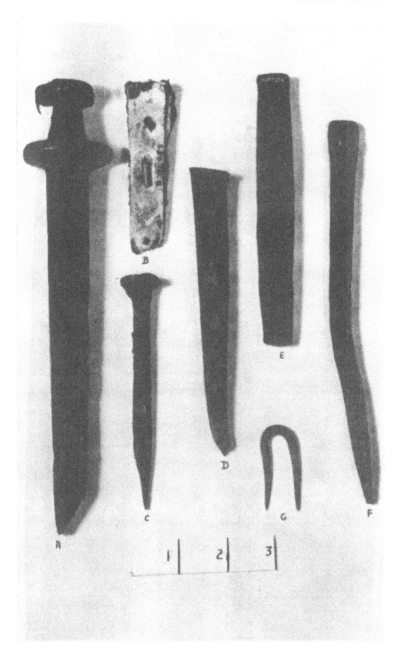

Iron chisels, perforated spikes and staple.

PLATE XXXIV

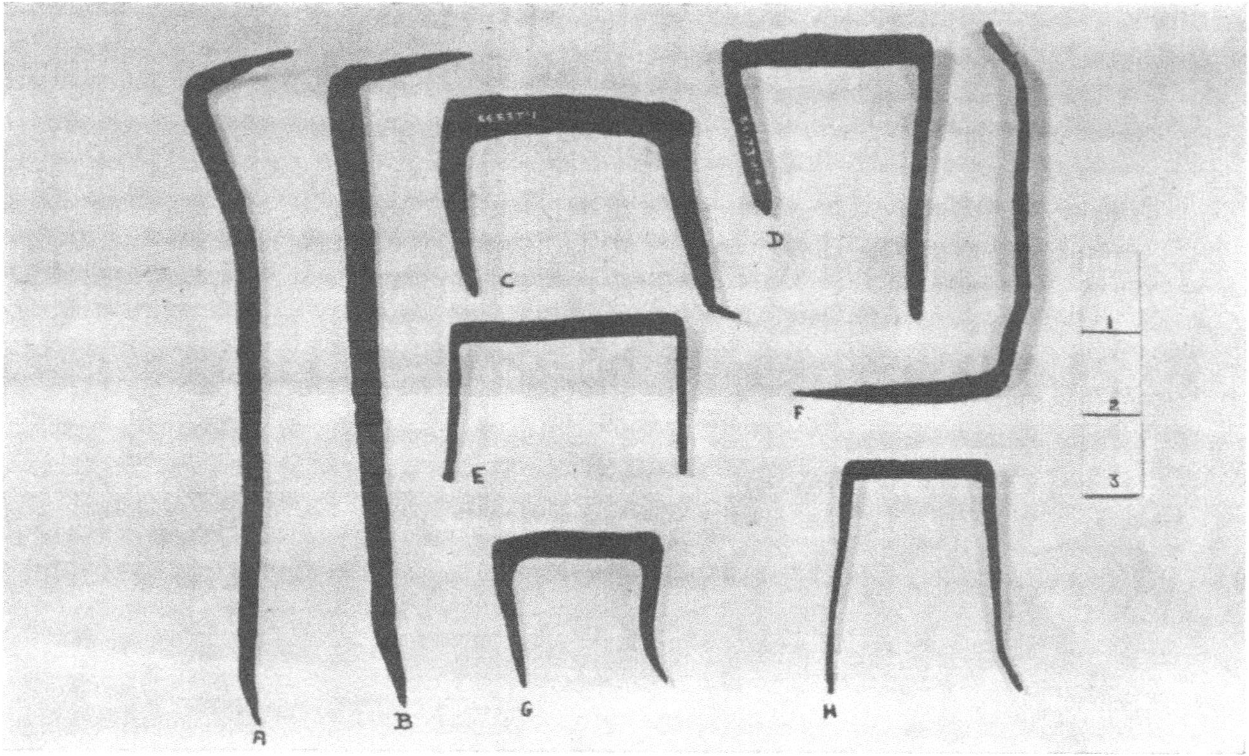

Iron clamps and angle-irons.

PLATE XXXV

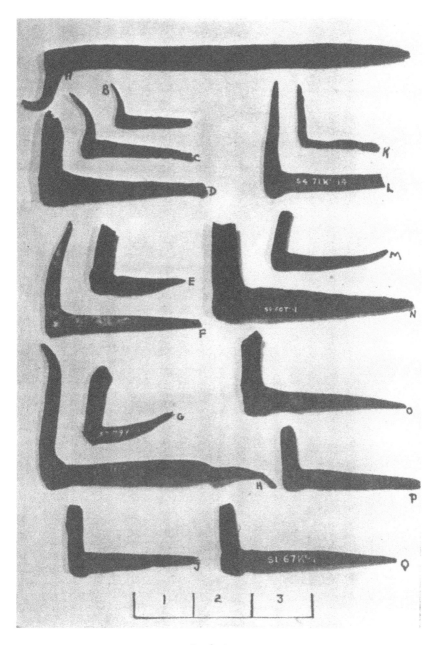

Angle-irons

PLATE XXXVI

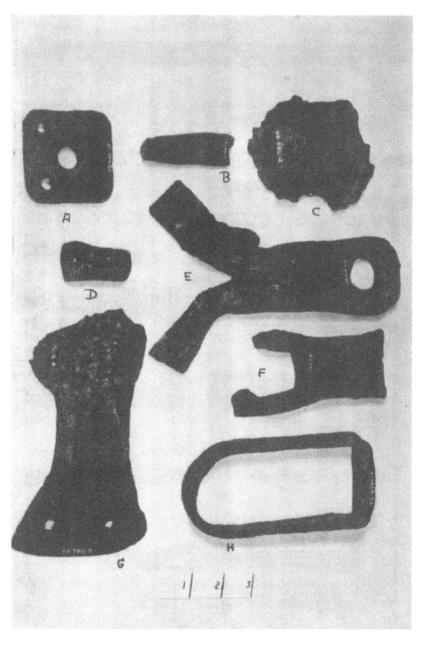

Masonry anchors, perforated iron objects and iron ingot.

PLATE XXXVII

Three concave iron disks.

PLATE XXXVIII

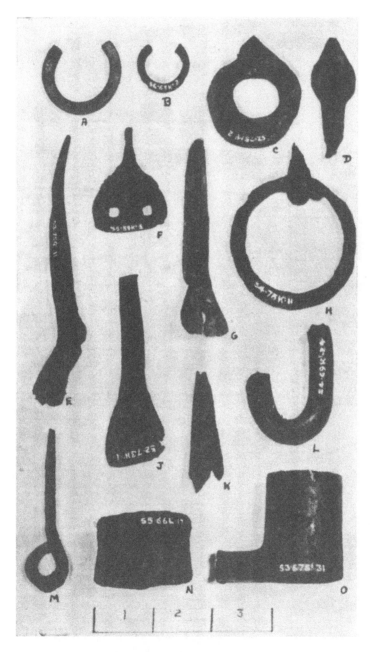

Iron rings, washers, latches, door swings, etc.

PLATE XXXIX

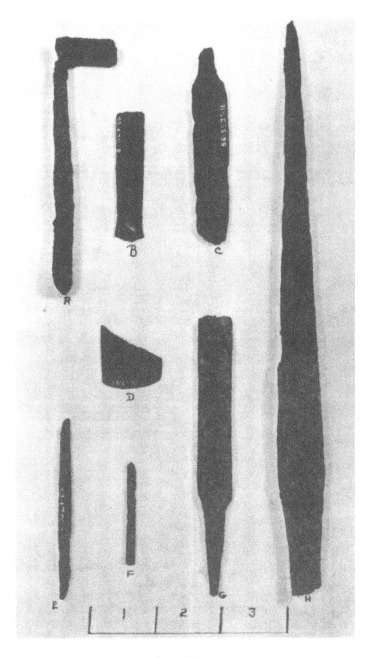

Iron files.

PLATE XL

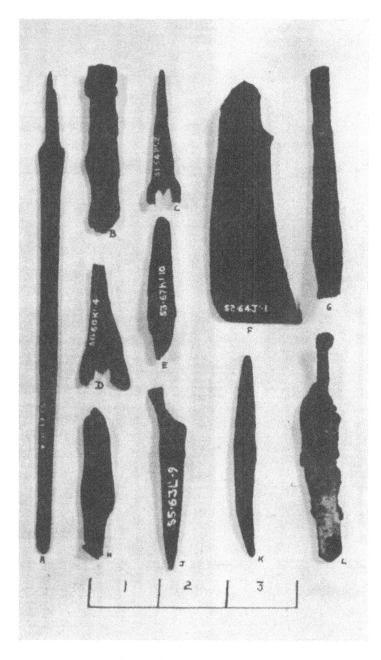

Screw-driver, claws, reamers, and hatchet.

PLATE XLI

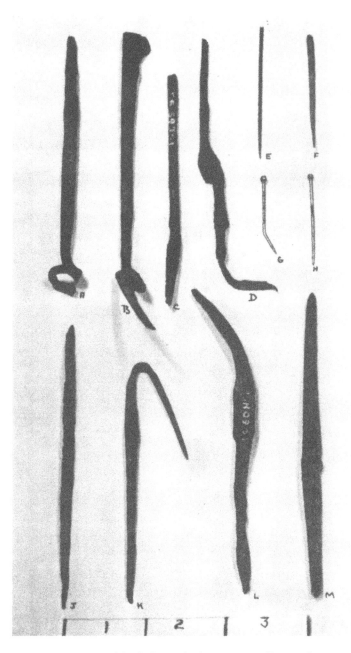

Screw, table fork, scalpel, pins, needles, and
double-pointed bars.

PLATE XLII

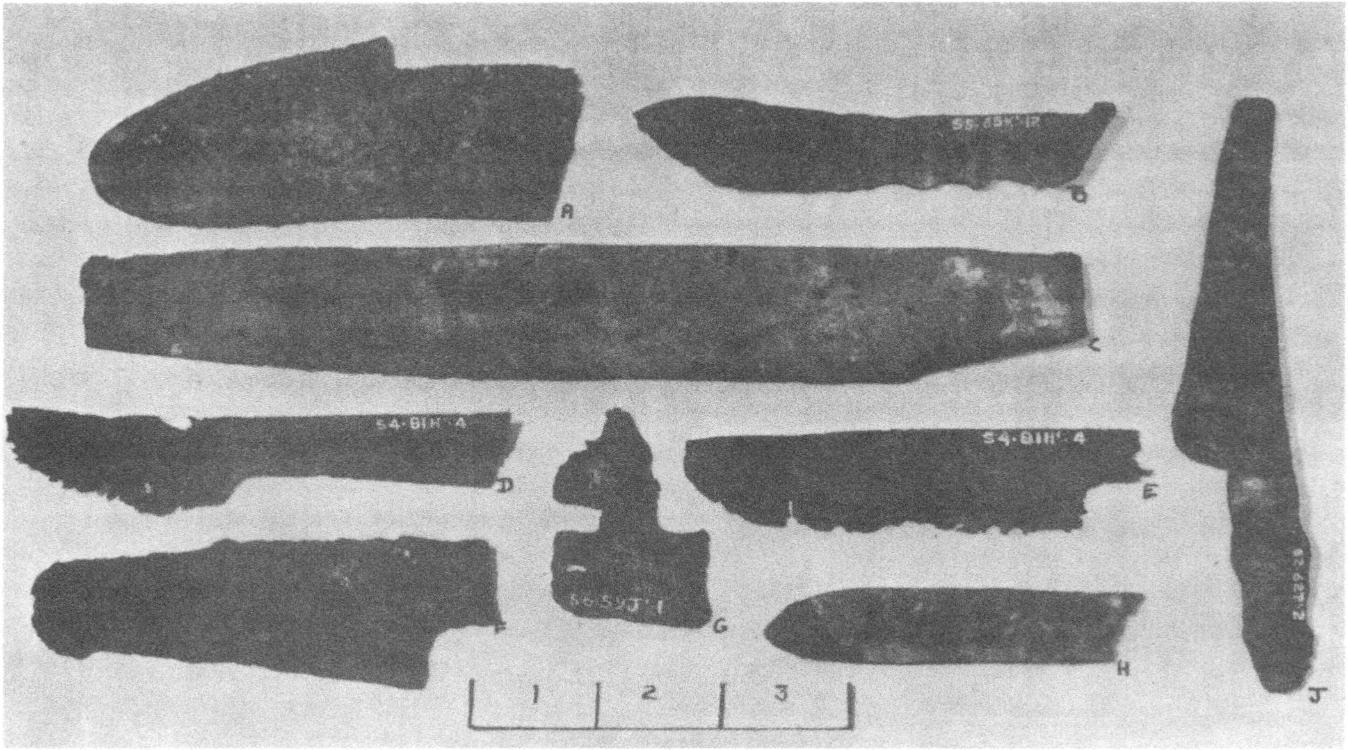

Draw-shave and iron knives.

PLATE XLIII

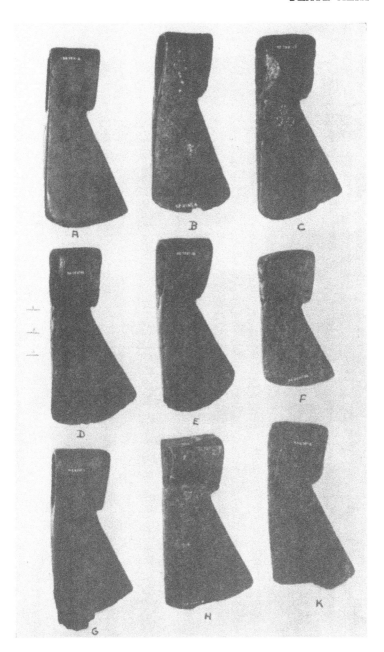

Iron axes.

PLATE XLIV

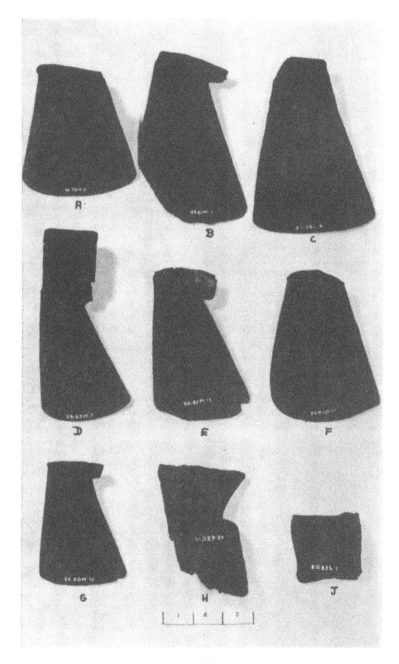

Broken iron axes.

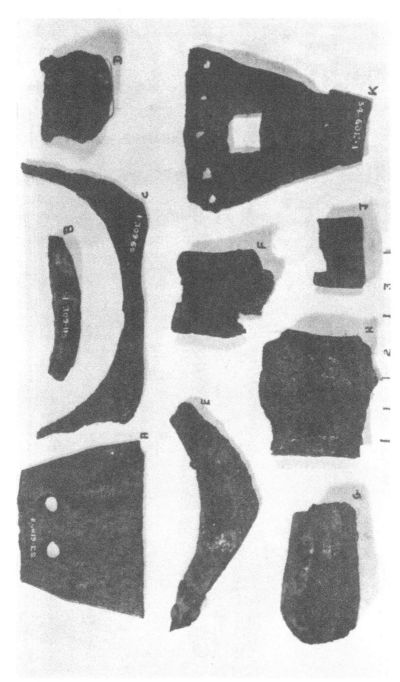

PLATE XLV

Perforated pieces of iron, ferrules and spring.

PLATE XLVI

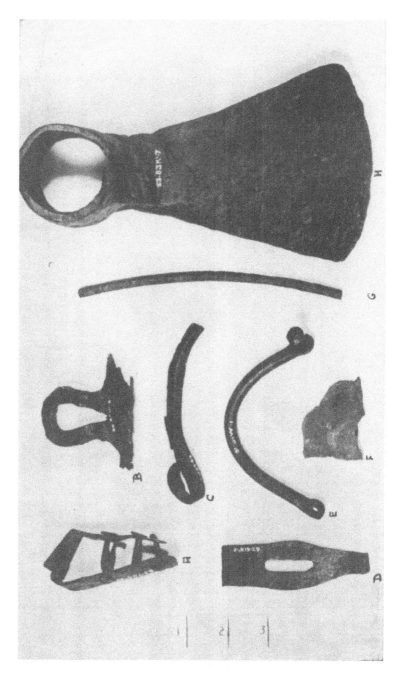

Iron adze, fragments of cooking pots, and specimens of unknown use.

PLATE XLVII

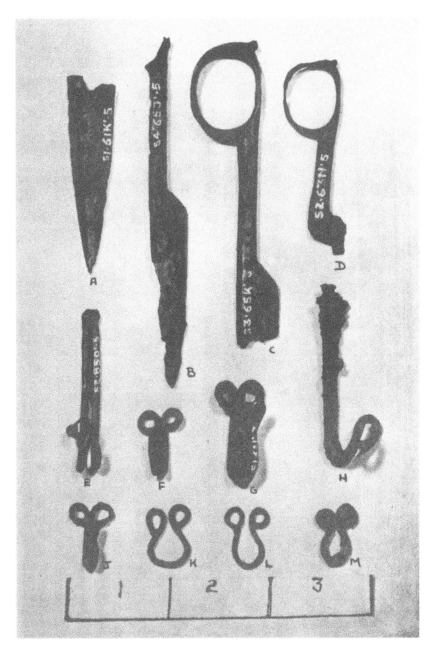

Fragments of scissors, hooks and eyes.

PLATE XLVIII

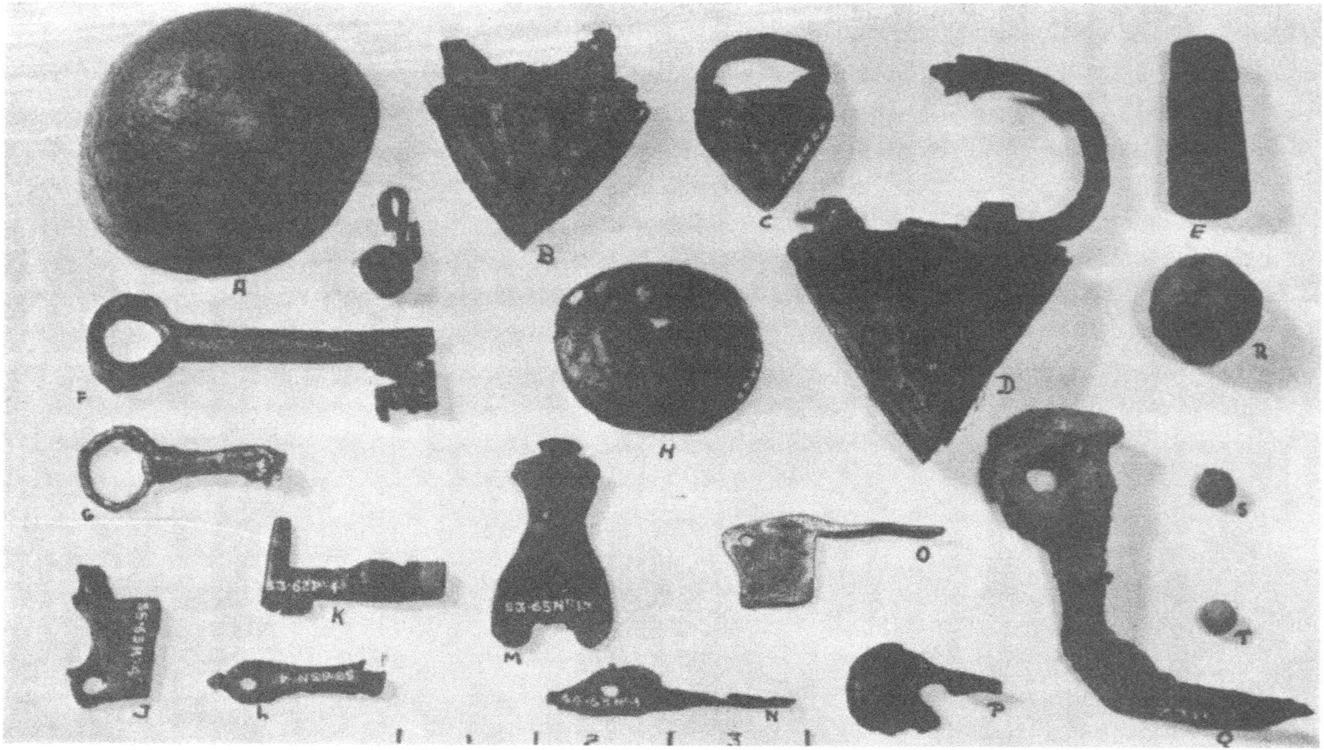

Bells, padlocks, gun parts and balls.

PLATE XLIX

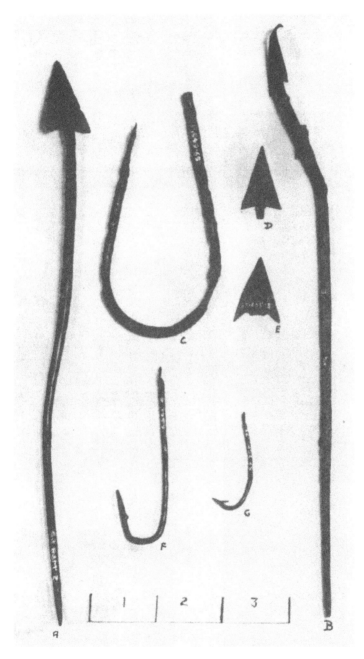

Iron points and fish-hooks.

PLATE L

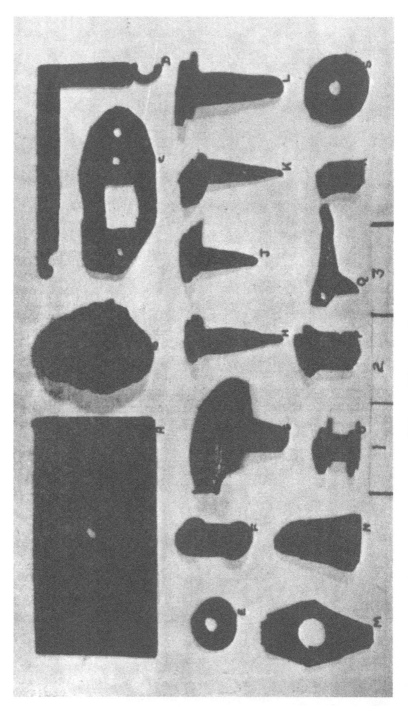

Objects of brass and copper.